PALEO
girl

LESLIE KLENKE

PRIMAL
BLUEPRINT
PUBLISHING

PALEO GIRL

Library of Congress Control Number: 2014905573
Library of Congress Cataloging-in-Publication Data is on file with the publisher
Klenke, Leslie, 1983-
Paleo Girl: Take a Leap. Empower Yourself. Be Awesome. / Leslie Klenke

ISBN: 978-1-939563-13-2
1. Self-Help 2. Health & Fitness 3. Body, Mind & Spirit

Editor: Elizabeth Mostaedi
Copy Editor: Amy Lucas
Consulting and Research: Adam Lambert, Vanessa Lambert, and Siena Colombier
Design and Layout: Leslie Klenke
Interior Photography: Jered Scott (Page 27), Calm Pictures and Ali Walker (Page 254)
Recipe and Fitness Photography: Leslie Klenke
Fitness Model: Olivia Weltsch

For more information about *Paleo Girl* and Primal Blueprint Publishing, please visit primalblueprintpublishing.com. For information on quantity discounts, please call 888-774-6259 or email: info@primalblueprint.com
Publisher: Primal Blueprint Publishing. 23805 Stuart Ranch Rd. Suite 145 Malibu, CA90265

Table of Contents

Acknowledgments

In the weeks and days leading up to the writing of these acknowledgments, I've found myself composing rough drafts in my mind: while I'm in the shower, cooking dinner, or lying wide awake at night. I've been *so* excited to thank everyone who's had a hand in this book coming to fruition, but I've also been slightly anxious about finding the right words to sincerely express my gratitude, and the immense emotion that would surely arise while searching for those words. You don't spend a year of your life exclusively putting your time and energy into a project like this and not experience a full spectrum of emotions, all of which are tied to the amazing individuals that helped *Paleo Girl* see the light of day. Yes, I came up with the concept, organized and researched the topics, shot much of my own photography, and designed the book from cover to cover—but I could never take credit for it all. *Paleo Girl* is the culmination of so many people's time, energy, and love. With that said, I'd like to say:

Thank you...

Mark Sisson, you believed in my vision for *Paleo Girl* and trusted I was the perfect person for the job. You've directly changed my life, and indirectly transformed the lives of so many people I love and care about. Thank you for being you.

Brad Kearns, your endless hours of editing, fact checking, guidance, and comic relief helped mold that original email into the book you hold in your hands today. Thank you so much for going on this wild ride with me.

Elizabeth Mostaedi, goodness. Where on Earth would we be without each other? I can't even begin to thank you for the time, dedication, and patience you've had with me throughout this past year—both mentally and spiritually. You are truly a gift in every part of my life and I am eternally grateful for you. *(Of course!)*

Amy Lucas, the best editor I could have asked for. You're probably surprised I ever passed an English class in my life! Thank you so much for helping me deliver my message and polishing it up for the world to enjoy.

Aaron Fox, Siena Colombier, Farhad Mostaedi, and the rest of the Primal Nutrition staff that supported this project in anyway...including keeping me entertained with silly internet videos, cuddly dogs, and bashing some Primal snacks when I'm in the office—thank you all.

Adam and Vanessa Lambert, thank you both so much for your endless knowledge and your passion to so willingly share it with others. I feel honored just knowing you two, let alone having your help with creating this book.

Sarah Grace Davis, who knew that in 2011 when you introduced me to MDA and *The Primal Blueprint* that such a beautiful chain of events would be set into motion? From that brief conversation, you ultimately helped create this book; assisted many of my friends and family to lose hundreds of pounds; and even facilitated a marriage! (Ahem…Elizabeth and Farhad Mostaedi.) Thank you so much for being my "ah ha" moment and for continually paying it forward.

Jenny Brenner, Chris Wilson, and Kyle Wilson, the unbelievable dedication and patience you've all had while finding true happiness and health has been nothing short of inspiring. I'm so proud of the work each of you have put in, and am so blessed to have such a loving and supportive family.

Teresa Klenke, my momma. From my first day on this planet I knew I was loved, and that's what's shaped me into the person I am today. I credit my happiness, open-mindedness, and passion for life to you. Thank you for every single ounce of support you've ever given me.

AJ Wilson, so this is what love really feels like. It's so much more dynamic and complex than I ever knew was possible. I'll never be able to thank you enough for the dedication, sacrifice, encouragement, strength, love, and endless help you've given me over this past year. As with anything, there were some ups and downs, but boy did we grow together. *That's* love.

Lastly, thank you to the rest of my amazing friends and family who never took my being a hermit for the past year personally, and for the infinite love and support. You all know who you are.

I first met Leslie Klenke at PrimalCon Ox-
nard in April 2013. She volunteered to help
prepare for the event with her close friend
and our Community Outreach Manager
Elizabeth Mostaedi. In our first casual interaction, I came to discover Leslie's amazing
array of writing, designing, and marketing
talents, and her passion for Primal living.
She let it slip that she had a dream of
writing a book for young women to promote
health and empowerment in the spirit of
the Primal Blueprint principles. I offered her
some words of encouragement and went
about my day.

You see, now that I'm a publisher, I get hit with a ton of book pitches—on air-
planes, at the supermarket—you know the drill. The truth is, lots of people dream
of writing a book but they might not have an interesting story to tell, or even the
writing skills to tell a proper story. I can tell after only a few minutes of reading a
proposal whether a book has some magic and excitement or not. In Hollywood,
they say the same thing about movies. Maybe you'll agree? Can you tell if the
movie you're watching is gonna be good after just a few minutes? Same thing for
a bad movie, you know? It starts out lame and never gets better!

Anyway, later that month after my discussion with Leslie, she emailed me an
incredible document that eventually became this book. Her *Paleo Girl* file was
more than just a bunch of facts about eating healthy, exercising sensibly, and doing some cool DIY stuff (I had to ask her what DIY stood for…now I see it all over
magazine covers and Internet sites…duh!). Her book was a journey of sharing
and connecting, and being vulnerable and honest and heartfelt. Leslie wrote this
book to entertain you, educate you, and maybe help you gain more happiness
and enjoyment during a time of life that might not always be easy.

It's kind of weird to think that this fancy, beautifully designed book you hold in
your hands was once just an email of a simple, plain Word doc. But Leslie had

a dream and she pursued it by working really hard and doing the very best she could to tell a powerful story directly to you, like she's sitting right there next to you. I hope you can appreciate all the fun and hard work and passion that went into this project, as all of us at Primal Blueprint Publishing have long dreamed about creating a book just for young readers. Finally, it's here. Enjoy!

Mark Sisson
Malibu, CA
April, 2014

Chapter One

Diet 101: The Skinny

What Is Paleo?

Paleo and Primal lifestyles mimic the way your ancestors lived 10,000 years ago. Are we talking caveman stuff here? Well, kind of! It's hard to imagine a world before texting and drive-thru burger joints, but shockingly there was one. A teenager living 10,000 years ago, let's call her Grokette, wasn't very different from the teenager you are today. Sure you dress differently, entertain yourself differently, and probably talk a lot differently, but on the inside, you and Grokette are pretty much the same.

You were never meant to sit in a chair all day, eat junk food, and barely go outside. You were built to move around, eat real food, and have fun in the sun! Don't get me wrong, technology is totally awesome, but in many ways, the convenience of modern life is making us all fat, sick, and unhappy.

I'm not saying you should put this book down and go live in a cave, but there are some simple steps you can take to model your life more around that of your primal ancestors. If you follow some of the basic guidelines in the pages that follow, you will become a happier and healthier teen because you'll be living the life you were programmed for.

What Is Primal Eating?

So what did Grokette eat? Her diet would have been dependent upon where she lived. If she was raised in the Amazon, she probably ate a lot of tropical fruits and vegetables. On the other hand, if she grew up in the Arctic, she most likely survived on animal meat. Regardless of sun or snow, what did these two different diets have in common? You guessed it...they both helped Grokette enjoy optimal health. If she were around today to show us a thing or two, she'd be much healthier than most of us. Crazy, right? Why? Because she ate whole, seasonally available foods rather than processed garbage typical of today's society.

Well, this isn't 10,000 years ago, and odds are you don't live in a rainforest or an igloo...so, what should you eat? The answer is simple: plants and animals. Hmm, that answer may be a little too basic, though. Let me explain with a more in-depth description of paleo foods.

Vegetables & Fruits

Veggies like broccoli, peppers, and onions are high in nutritional value and antioxidants, which are agents that help the cells inside your body fight infection and disease. Fruits like strawberries, raspberries, and blueberries are also high in antioxidants and have low-glycemic values. This means they are less sugary, so they don't spike your energy quickly with a "sugar high." They provide a more stable source of energy that helps you avoid those awful sugar crashes that strike when you drink soda or eat candy.

Animal Protein & Eggs

Basic animal proteins include meat (beef and pork), fowl (chicken and turkey), and fish. These items, along with eggs, provide healthy sources of protein, saturated fats (which many people believe are unhealthy but are actually a great source of energy and only cause damage when combined with too many processed carbohydrates), omega-3 fats (which are good for your heart and are anti-inflammatory), and vitamins.

Healthy Fats & Oils

Healthy fats are some of the most nutritious foods in existence. Consuming "good" fat helps you absorb the nutrients present in other foods that require fat for full absorption. Oils can also be used to boost your intake of omega-3s and other essential fatty acids. The healthiest fats and oils are animal fats, avocados/avocado oil, coconut oil, cod liver oil, egg yolks, grass-fed butter/ghee, olive oil, and palm oil.

It sounds like gossip, right?

In Moderation: Nuts & Dark Chocolate

Nuts such as macadamias, cashews, and almonds are packed with protein, antioxidants, vitamins, and minerals, and have less omega-6 than other nuts like walnuts do. (FYI: peanuts are *legumes,* not nuts. Avoid them!) Dark chocolate contains healthy fats like cocoa butter, it can lower your blood pressure, and there's even proof it can protect you from UV damage. Just be sure to eat good quality, high-cacao dark chocolate (70 percent or higher) and not milk or white chocolates.

Eating Fat DOESN'T Make You Fat!

Wait a minute! Animal protein, eggs, nuts, and oils…are you insane? No, I'm not, but you're not either for thinking that fat will make you fat. Get ready for this: we've been lied to. And I don't mean that your parents or health teachers have lied to you. Someone they trusted—ahem, the United States government—lied to them first. To be fair, a lot of these people didn't know they were lying. More often than not, trusted experts (like doctors, nutritionists, and even scientists) are misled by power players in the world of food and health. Part of a vicious cycle, this bad information gets passed on over and over until everyone thinks it's true.

Does this scenario seem familiar? I bet you've experienced the exact same thing on a much smaller scale. It sounds like gossip, right? People spreading rumors they heard from someone else, even if they have no clue if it's true. People gossip for a lot of reasons, don't they? Teens might gossip to feel better about themselves by putting someone down or trying to get even with a person or group they feel excluded from. When it comes to gossip in the world of nutrition, a lot of people say what's always been said (even if it's wrong) because they're afraid they might lose their jobs or ruin their reputations. Beware of gossip everywhere!

The truth is, fat is your friend. Fats that you get from animals and the healthy sources listed in the previous section not only keep you fuller for longer, but they also:

- Help you burn fat instead of sugar for fuel, because fat is your body's preferred energy source.
- Do not create insulin spikes.
- Help you absorb important vitamins like A, D, E, and K.
- Protect vital organs—yup, your body needs a little padding.
- Bottom line: the brain is 60 percent fat, so you do the math!

Are there such things as unhealthy fats? Absolutely. Not all fats are created equal—a really important fact to understand. Synthetically manufactured fats such as partially hydrogenated fats, trans fats, and fats from processed foods should be avoided at all costs. These fats are created from unnatural processes and are rendered unrecognizable to your body, thus wreaking havoc on your insides and screwing up your metabolism. Some scary things these fats can do are:

- Trigger systemic inflammation: an unhealthy swelling of all the tissues in your body. (This can make you look puffy. Eek!)
- Create an imbalance in your omega-6:omega-3 ratio.
- Promote weight (fat) gain.
- Speed the aging process.
- Cause cancer.

Does this mean you can eat all the healthy fats you want and never gain weight? Essentially yes, within reason, but there are two additional macronutrients you must consider: protein and carbohydrates. You will not experience any fat gain while consuming fat, as long as these three macronutrients are balanced.

Carbs: Are They the Enemy?

If you were to completely remove all carbohydrates from your diet, you would essentially be excluding a lot of yummy vegetables and fruits that are full of vitamins and minerals. The carbs you need to ditch are those found in:

- Legumes: beans, lentils, chickpeas, split peas, soybeans.
- Grains and starches: barley, corn, oats, rice, rye, wheat.
- Processed foods: bread, cake, cereals, cookies, crackers, pasta, soda, etc. (I could rattle on forever here, but I'm pretty sure you get the point!)

Hopefully this list doesn't look like your daily menu, but if it does, have no fear... help is on the way! These carbohydrates are on the naughty list because they spike your insulin, promote inflammation, can trigger depression, make you feel lazy, and flat out make you FAT!

Mark Sisson, author of *The Primal Blueprint* and the genius behind the Primal movement explains: "Carbohydrates cause insulin to increase; insulin increase causes you to store fat." So keep that in mind the next time you sink your teeth into a bagel. Even if the nutritional label says zero grams of fat and zero grams of sugar, once that processed bread goes into your body, it's broken down into glucose (sugar), causes a spike in your insulin, and eventually turns into fat if it's not burned off immediately. Who has time to run a marathon every time they eat a bowl of mac and cheese? I know I don't.

Your body turns sugar into fat.

Remember that Grokette wasn't eating donuts to survive. That's not to say she wouldn't have taken advantage of the convenience had some pastries been lying around (it would have been a whole heck of a lot easier to crack open a box of donuts than to chase down a wild beast), but it doesn't change the fact that your body just doesn't know what to do with grains and processed foods, and therefore treats them like poison.

Mmm...Protein

Ah yes, protein. Nothing like a juicy burger (hold the bun) hot off the grill! Protein is crucial for building muscle, it's digested slowly (which keeps you fuller for longer), and it doesn't cause insulin spikes. Not to mention, it's just plain delicious! Building muscle is important, because lean mass protects your body and helps you look fit; plus, the existence of muscle in your body burns more calories. So, the more muscle you have, the more efficient you are at burning fat. Pretty awesome, right?

The Lowdown on Omegas

Okay, I've been blabbing on and on about omegas…but what are they? For starters, there are five different kinds of omegas: omega-3, -5, -6, -7, and -9. Omega-3 (anti-inflammatory) and omega-6 (pro-inflammatory) are the only omegas known to be essential to humans. They're considered essential because your body doesn't actually create them on its own, so it's your job to be sure you eat the right kinds of foods to obtain them. The lesser known omega-5, -7, and -9 are classified as "conditionally essential," meaning your body doesn't need them unless you have some type of disease or developmental condition. The typical American eats way too many omega-6s, and far too few omega-3s. A lot of this discrepancy is due to the hidden omega-6 content in the vegetable and seed oils that are commonly found in the Standard American Diet (SAD). The ideal omega-6:omega-3 ratio is 1:1; however, this is nearly impossible to accomplish in our modern society that runs on a diet of junk food and late night drive-thru binges. Grokette easily met this dietary ratio because plants and animals were not highly processed, treated with pesticides and chemicals, or raised on commercial farms.

If the "conventional" food most of us eat today is not as nutritionally dense and lacks crucial components like healthy omega-3s, how are you supposed to bridge the gap? Try incorporating more animal proteins like grass-fed livestock and fish, or foods like macadamia nuts, grass-fed butter, avocados, and coconut oil. Eliminating vegetable and seed oils found in fried foods from fast food restaurants and the "snack aisle" at the grocery will also help balance those omegas in no time.

What Is Organic?

Grokette and the rest of our ancestors hunted wild prey that roamed freely, and they gathered fruits, vegetables, nuts, and seeds that grew naturally in their indigenous environments. Fast forward to today and we find large agriculture companies running the show. Our land is filled with massive commercial farms and crops. Honestly, without the Agricultural Revolution (the change from hunting and gathering to a civilized lifestyle, where people grew crops and stayed in one place instead of constantly searching for food), there's a chance many of us wouldn't be here today. Agriculture certainly has helped prevent widespread starvation in the world during times of crisis; however, it has come at a cost to our health.

On most commercial farms, animals are fed an unnatural diet of grains to plump them up so farmers can make a larger profit. (If people know grains make animals fat, shouldn't they realize that grains make people fat too? Duh.) Animals fed these unnatural diets are also given hormones (which make them grow faster), as well as antibiotics (because you can't have that many animals in one place without wide spread disease). All of these terrible things that go into the diet of a commercially raised animal ultimately go into your stomach bite by bite. Do you really want to dine on swine growth hormones for dinner tonight? Yeah, I didn't think so.

Growth hormones for dinner, anyone?

ORGANIC
FARM

Please
DO NOT
SPRAY

Our crops aren't safe anymore either. The chemicals sprayed on plants to make them grow faster and the pesticides/herbicides used to kill all the bugs and weeds soak into the produce. Again, these harmful chemicals end up in your body. Doesn't that just make your mouth water? Umm, probably not.

You have eaten more growth hormones, antibiotics, pesticides, and chemicals than I can even calculate. (Don't worry, I have too. We all have.) It just goes back to conventional wisdom; gossip that these farm chemicals are safe when they really aren't (or at least we're not sure they are safe). I didn't tell you all of this to freak you out, though. Use this information as knowledge to make better choices moving forward.

With all that said, what does organic mean? Organic tosses all the horrifying stuff I just discussed out the window. Organically raised, grass-fed or pastured animals survive on their naturally preferred diet and are not injected with a cocktail of manmade potions. Organically grown produce is not treated with compounds that only belong in a science lab. Instead, organic fruits and vegetables are cultivated as naturally as possible. These are "clean foods" that do not put any mystery items in your system. You (or your parents) should buy organically raised meat and produce as often as budget and availability allow. Yes, organic food can be a little (or a lot) more expensive than non-organic food, but the health benefits are way worth it.

Non-conventionally raised animals and animal products fall under a number of categories:

> • Cage-Free/Free-Range: commonly found on egg labels, cage-free means chickens were not confined to cages. These chickens live in an open barn but do not generally have access outside. Free-range chickens are able to go outside, but there are no regulations on the amount, duration, or quality of outdoor access.

- Grass-Fed/Grass-Finished: animals that are grass-fed are raised on a forage diet. Sometimes grass-fed animals are moved to a feedlot for "grain-finishing," but grass-finished animals remain on a pasture their entire life.

- Organically Raised: poultry, cattle, and pigs that are organically raised live on organic pastures, are fed organic feed their entire lives, are not given drugs, antibiotics, or growth hormones, and have year-round outdoor access.

- Pasture-Raised: animals roam freely in their natural environment and consume a natural diet. Pasturing improves the welfare of the animal, helps reduce environmental damage, and yields higher quality products that taste better and are more nutritious than conventional products.

- Wild Caught: fish that are raised in their natural habitat are wild caught, as opposed to farm-raised fish that live in compact tanks, are fed fishmeal from conventionally grown crops, and receive antibiotics. Farm-raised fish meat is often gray, so artificial dye is added to make the fish look more appealing to consumers.

One of the best (and most fun) places to buy organic foods is at local farms or farmers markets. When you go to a farmers market, the prices are probably going to be about the same as the prices at your local grocery store; the difference is the "big chain" stuff is typically grown far away with chemicals, and is not nearly as good for you. Once produce is harvested, it begins to lose nutrients. Instead of eating fruits and veggies that have traveled days (and sometimes weeks) to get to you, opt for local produce with a higher nutritional content.

Nutrition aside, farmers markets are great environments to hang out, get some sun and fresh air, and give back to your community. You can't get much more Primal unless you grow the produce yourself!

Let's recap: Yes, organic is better than commercially grown or conventional food, but sometimes it's hard to find. And yes, occasionally it's not just a little more expensive; it's a lot more expensive. But I don't want you to stress about having everything you eat be the best, most perfect choice. In fact, there are certain conventional fruits and veggies that are perfectly acceptable to eat.

Non-Organic Approved Produce	Organic Approved Produce
• Asparagus	• Apple
• Avocado	• Berries (blueberry, raspberry)
• Banana	• Celery
• Broccoli	• Cucumber
• Cantaloupe	• Cherries
• Grapefruit	• Grapes
• Kiwi Fruit	• Leafy Greens (Spinach, Kale)
• Mango	• Nectarine
• Mushroom	• Peach
• Onion	• Pear
• Papaya	• Sweet Bell Peppers
• Pineapple	• Summer Squash/Zucchini

There are two reasons why some produce is okay to eat non-organic and others aren't. One is the fruit or vegetable's skin. Look at onions and pineapple. The outer skin, or rind, keeps the food inside safe from chemical spraying and is simply removed before eating. Items like berries or leafy greens, on the other hand, cannot be peeled. For this reason, you can't remove the part that was exposed to pesticides, and most of the time the produce is too soft to be thoroughly washed or scrubbed. The second reason is all about bugs and their picky appetites. Foods like asparagus and mushrooms just don't taste good to most pests, so they don't eat them. That means farmers don't have to use as many (or any) chemicals on these crops.

Who knew bugs were picky eaters?

So Now What?

Fats: check. Carbs: check. Protein: check. Now, where do you go from here? You may be suffering from a bit of information overload, but you now have the groundwork done to start eating paleo!

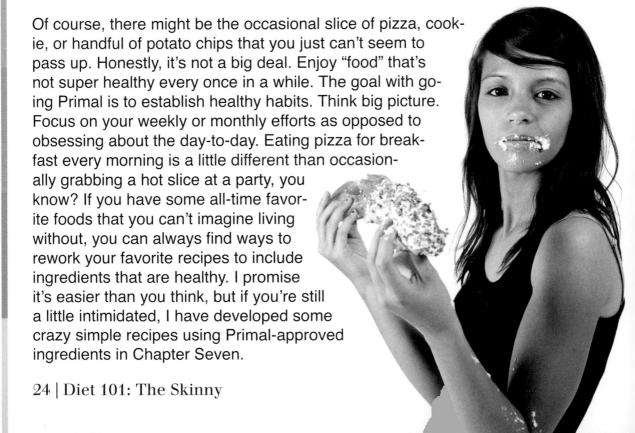

If you're thinking, "Great, does this mean I'll never be able to eat any of my favorite foods again?" The answer is—of course not! The key is to start adapting small changes into your lifestyle in order to begin promoting health and longevity. If you're a junk food junkie, try replacing some of your unhealthy snacks or meals with healthy, minimally processed ones. The beauty of real, whole foods is that once your body gets a taste, you will actually stop craving all those disease-promoting processed foods. The garbage that most teenagers eat every day— without a thought as to what they're putting in their bodies—will acutally start tasting like garabage. Real food has that effect!

Of course, there might be the occasional slice of pizza, cookie, or handful of potato chips that you just can't seem to pass up. Honestly, it's not a big deal. Enjoy "food" that's not super healthy every once in a while. The goal with going Primal is to establish healthy habits. Think big picture. Focus on your weekly or monthly efforts as opposed to obsessing about the day-to-day. Eating pizza for breakfast every morning is a little different than occasionally grabbing a hot slice at a party, you know? If you have some all-time favorite foods that you can't imagine living without, you can always find ways to rework your favorite recipes to include ingredients that are healthy. I promise it's easier than you think, but if you're still a little intimidated, I have developed some crazy simple recipes using Primal-approved ingredients in Chapter Seven.

If you're sitting there saying to yourself, "Leslie, this makes sense and all, but right now I can eat whatever I want, not gain any weight, and I feel fine. Why should I care about any of this?"

Do you want the honest answer? Because you won't always be able to get away with this crap! Have you ever heard of the Freshman 15? It refers to how many students gain 15 pounds (or more) of fat the first year they go to college. They have freedom for the first time, and they live in dorms where they can eat whatever they want on campus (like a kid in a candy store…literally). They're probably drinking alcohol (which can cause excess weight gain and bloating) and eating tons of pizza and junk food at parties. Did you know, by the time you go to college, you have pretty much stopped growing? This means you no longer need the same amount of calories that you did during your final growth spurt in your teen years. But when you run off to college, your fun new life typically has you chowing down more calories than ever, and often times from easy-to-grab processed food. Add all this up and it's easy to put on extra fat. Let me tell you, college is hard enough without having to feel bad about outgrowing your favorite jeans from senior year.

The Freshman 15 is super easy to put on, but it's a nightmare to take off. In fact, it's especially hard for girls whose metabolisms slow down as they stop growing. If they get a little heavy when they're teenagers, they tend to stay that way for years. That's why, even if things seem fine right now, you should look at this book as an opportunity to get ahead. If you start today, you won't have to spend years repairing the damage that you could potentially cause if you continue on an unhealthy path. Help your body achieve optimal health and endless energy, and look amazing while doing it now! The adult you're on your way to becoming will thank you for it!

You won't always get away with this crap!

I went to college at Bowling Green State University (BGSU) in northern Ohio. Go Falcons! I had already packed on some pounds from a few years at community college in my hometown of Dayton, Ohio before even starting at BGSU. I had always been in great shape in high school, but once I had a crazy schedule packed full of classes and parties, I started to gain weight. Once I left Dayton to go to BGSU, I decided I needed to get my weight under control, but unfortunately, I didn't know what "healthy" really meant.

I was in love with the coffee shop on campus and often ordered fat-free, sugar-free drinks I thought were healthy. I ate a ton of whole grains and prepackaged frozen "healthy" meals. I was able to shed some weight, but it was at the cost of my health and energy. I became exhausted. On days I didn't have class, I would sleep all day. I had a hard time focusing during lectures and on homework and exams. Not to mention, I was always hungry, which often led to binging at the burrito place across the street from my apartment.

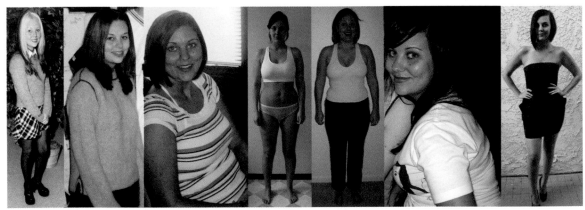

The evolution of a yo-yo dieter. From left to right: Senior year 2001 Homecoming Court (check out that hair!), 115 lbs; December 2002 and a total brace face, 130 lbs; June 2005 (horizontal stripes were not my friend), 142 lbs; May 2006 after months of calorie-restricted dieting (can you see how tired I am?), 125 lbs; January 2007 smiling on the outside, 145 lbs; August 2008 and my highest weight when I first moved to Los Angeles, 155 lbs; May 2011 after figuring out what my body actually needs, a happy and healthy 125 lbs.

By the end of my first year I miraculously hit my goal weight, but gained it all back (all 17 pounds of it and then some) my first summer back home. I repeated this same pattern the following year. I spent more time yo-yoing than I'd like to admit. I caused some serious damage to my health, my metabolism, and my self-esteem over that time. It wasn't until I moved to Los Angeles, California and discovered the Primal lifestyle that I was finally able to get the weight off…and keep it off. I have more energy now than I did when I was in college, I feel confident in the way I look, and I have a healthy relationship with food.

I only wish someone could have helped me understand this process when I was in college (or sooner). I could have avoided years of struggle, and I wouldn't have had to work so hard trying to shed the pounds I'd gained from eating what conventional wisdom tricked me into believing was healthy. So I mean it when I say: you are a young, vibrant, and beautiful girl who holds a world of information in her hands—info I'd have killed to have when I was your age. Make this work for you. Don't fight like I did. Eat real food. Be happy. Be your best YOU.

Me at my current weight in 2014—and no more yo-yo dieting! I don't weigh myself all that often now, because that number really means nothing to me. I'm healthier than I've ever been and that's what matters the most. *Photo credit: Jered Scott*

What Is Paleo?

A paleo or Primal lifestyle, like the one Grokette lived, is one that attempts to mimic (as closely as you can, and within reason) the lives of our hunter-gatherer ancestors who lived 10,000 years ago, before the Agricultural Revolution. The best part is that you don't need to live in a cave to reprogram your body and achieve optimal health!

What Is Primal eating?

Primal eating focuses on:

- Vegetables & Fruits: For their high nutritional value, antioxidants, and low-glycemic values that don't create large insulin spikes.
- Animal Protein & Eggs: For their healthy sources of protein, fat, omega-3s, and vitamins.
- Healthy Fat & Oils: Not only because they are some of the most nutrient-dense foods, but also because they help you absorb nutrients in other foods and give you a serious boost of omega-3s.
- Nuts & Dark Chocolate: Can be consumed in moderation. Most nuts are packed with protein, antioxidants, vitamins, and minerals. Dark chocolate (70 percent or higher) contains healthy fat, it can lower your blood pressure, and may protect you from UV damage.

Eating fat DOESN'T make you fat!

The consumption of healthy fats will not make you fat. That belief is part of "conventional wisdom" and is pretty much gossip. Healthy fats from animal and vegetable sources are an excellent supply of energy for your body, while unhealthy fats that are manmade are essentially like poison. Additionally, healthy fats keep you full and keep your food intake in check.

Carbs: Are They the Enemy?

Carbs from natural foods like vegetables and fruits are great sources of vitamins and minerals. The types of carbs you need to cut back on or eliminate are:

- Legumes: beans, lentils, chickpeas, split peas, soybeans.
- Grains and starches: barley, corn, oats, rice, rye, wheat.
- Processed foods: bread, cake, cereals, cookies, crackers, pasta, soda, etc.

Mmm…Protein

Protein helps you build muscle, is digested slowly, and doesn't cause insulin spikes. Muscles protect your body, help you look fit, and burn calories. The best sources of protein in your diet are animal meats, eggs, fish, nuts, and seeds.

The Lowdown on Omegas

Two important types of omega fatty acids are omega-3s and omegas-6s. Omega-3s are anti-inflammatory (help prevent inflammation), while omega-6s are pro-inflammatory (actually promote inflammation). The ideal omega-6:omega-3 ratio in your diet should be 1:1—getting the same amount of each. Most people eating the Standard American Diet (SAD) get way too many omega-6s (from junk food, vegetable oils, and other processed foods), and way too little omega-3s (found in meat and healthy fats). You can help improve your omega-6:omega-3 ratio by including more paleo foods in your diet.

What Is Organic?

Organically raised meats and organically grown produce are not treated with growth hormones, antibiotics, pesticides, herbicides, or other gross chemicals. They are what we call "clean foods" and you should eat them as often as they are available or budget allows.

So Now What?

You have now passed the course on "Diet 101: The Skinny" and have laid the groundwork for eating paleo. So, bust out that workout gear—up next in Chapter Two you will learn about Primal fitness!

My Freshman (More than) 15

Learn from the mistakes I made after spending years yo-yo dieting; instead make smart decisions using the knowledge you gain from this book. I would have killed for this information when I was your age. Eat real food. Be happy. Be your best YOU.

Chapter Two

Fitness 101: Work It Girl!

What Is Primal Fitness?

Let's check back in with our Primal rockstar, Grokette. Yes, she was super fit, I promise you that, but how do I know? Consider this: her fitness was literally a matter of life or death. She and her family had to hunt for meals, gather fruits and vegetables, collect firewood, run from predators, and travel by foot wherever they wanted to go. Thanks to Grokette and the rest of our ancestors, the human body has evolved to move in amazing ways. Believe it or not, you're a natural athlete! However, when you get too caught up in a modern lifestyle, you can become lazy and out of shape, and fall into a sedentary routine.

What this means for the modern day Grokette is that you need to make a special effort to not only get enough exercise, but to also get the right kinds of exercise that your body depends on to be healthy. Obviously, you don't need to do the exact same activities your Primal ancestors engaged in. I mean do you really want to spend your Friday night getting chased by a saber-toothed tiger or lifting rocks to build a shelter after a long day of scrounging for food? Yeah, that's not exactly how I like to start my weekend either. But here's the cool part—you can model your exercise in the spirit of your ancestors and choose workouts that have a similar effect on your body. The benefits of Primal-style exercise include:

- A more efficient metabolism—burn fat better.
- A more regulated appetite—no more sugar crashes and binges.
- An awesome stress management tool. (As you've probably already discovered!)
- Better oxygen delivery to your heart and lungs.
- Stronger muscles, bones, joints, and connective tissues.
- Better immune system function—get sick less often.
- Better function of all your organs.
- Release of natural "feel good" hormones—like a natural high.

You may be thinking, "My friends all have workout DVDs and do hours of cardio; is that what I should be doing?" Sure, if you want to spend hours in agony doing "chronic cardio," be my guest! Conventional wisdom probably has you fooled into believing that you need to spend a chunk of your day on a treadmill or in an aerobics class to achieve your physical goals. (Don't feel bad…I was victim of this crap too!) When in doubt, ask yourself WWGD? (What would Grokette do?) Do you think she worked herself to death to get in shape? Of course not! Working out at those levels would have exhausted her, made her easy prey, and prevented her from being able to hunt/gather her next meal. She stayed in shape naturally because she allowed her genes to function the way they were meant to by eating and being naturally active.

Unlike gung-ho fitness peeps today that push themselves too hard due to peer pressure or maybe a psycho coach, gym teacher, or personal trainer screaming in their ears, those who practice natural exercise stay aligned with their attitudes and motivation levels. That's right, I hereby give you permission to rest your body when you're tired, feeling a little under the weather, or simply don't feel like doing your typical workout routine. I know it sounds too good to be true, but it's not!

Can someone please wake her up?

Chronic cardio (doing workouts at medium-to-high intensity that last too long and are done too frequently with insufficient rest in between) can do more damage than good. Yup, over-exercising could be worse for you than sitting on your couch. Scientists have observed countless drawbacks from chronic cardio, including:

- Overuse injuries from repetitive strain or cumulative trauma injuries like tendonitis, tennis elbow, or shin splints to name a few.

- Overstress. (Especially when you factor in all the other crazy stresses of life, like school, parents, and that annoying show-off at basketball practice!)

- Excess production of cortisol, a hormone that signals your body to break down muscle and store fat, specifically in the abdomen and around your organs. (If you're killing yourself in the gym and still can't see those abs, this could be why!)

- Burn sugar instead of fat as a fuel source.

- Trigger burnout or lack of motivation. (What good is a workout that you don't actually stick to?)

- Exhaustion—remember, the whole point of working out is to give you more energy during the day, not less!

But don't chuck your workout DVDs or cancel your monthly gym membership just yet. You should only get rid of exercise endeavors you're not approaching in a Primal manner or that you just can't stand doing. Is that DVD over an hour of high intensity, non-stop jumping, kicking, and punching? Then maybe it's time to replace it with something shorter and more realistic. Is your gym membership really an hour and a half of you sitting on a stationary bike catching up on your favorite gossip magazines? Then it's definitely time to refocus your time (and your money...even if it's your parent's!) into something that's actually going to give you results. So what the heck are you supposed to do? Oh, I'm so happy you asked!

The answer is way easier than you think:

- Move everyday at a comfortable pace (i.e., lots of walking).
- Lift heavy things (could even be your own body weight).
- Sprint once a week (but only for a short burst of time).

Seem to easy? Let me break it down for you.

Move Everyday

Be honest here, how active are you? If your days currently consist of hours of sitting at school, followed by hours of lounging at home, and ending with hours of laying in bed, the answer is: NOT ENOUGH. It's time to spice things up! I'm not talking about high intensity, run until your legs fall off every single day kind of effort; instead your goal should be to reach 55 to 75 percent of your maximum heart rate a couple hours every week. If you're not up to speed with heart rate training, the 55 to 75 percent range is actually super easy to get into. If you aren't all that fit right now, you can get there just by walking briskly. No joke, a walk can actually be considered a workout, and one that is healthier than the crazy intense, music-blasting group classes at the gym!

That's not so tough now, is it? Try incorporating some of these ideas:

- Walk or ride your bike to/from school (if you live close enough) instead of taking the bus or getting a ride.

- Grab a group of girlfriends and take a walk on your lunch break instead of chitchatting at the lunch table the whole period.

- Hit up the local skating rink and get some fun cardio in on the weekends instead of going to the movies.

- Find a hiking trail close to your home and plan an adventure with your friends instead of hitting up that fro-yo shop again.

- Go to the mall instead of shopping online. (Yes, someone is finally going to count your shopping habits as exercise!) Walk to as many stores as possible, be sure to take the stairs instead of elevators/escalators, and avoid the scary "food" in the food court. Who knew the mall could be your own personal (and free) gym?

Incorporating just a couple of those simple ideas, you will easily be able to hit your goal of two to five hours of moderate movement per week. Not sure you're getting enough? Check out the app store on your phone. Search "walk" and literally thousands of apps will pop up. These apps can help you track your time, distance, speed, route, and more—but only if you want to keep track of all those little details.

Do You Even Lift, Bro?

Aren't you sick of hearing all the boys brag about lifting? I know I am...so I decided to join them. Lifting isn't just for guys and it certainly won't bulk you up like a bodybuilder since you likely lack the high levels of male hormones in your bloodstream that cause muscles to get huge. Lifting heavy things helps you build sleek, toned muscles to make you stronger and leaner, and to energize you more than any energy drink could.

It doesn't get easier, you get better.

Picture yourself 10,000 years ago. If you needed something heavy moved, you moved it. Grokette didn't have equipment or machines to do it for her. If she needed something substantial relocated, she put forth great effort for a short period of time, then rested once the task was accomplished. This is the same type of Primal movement you should incorporate into your lifestyle. You don't need to run outside and pick up boulders anytime soon (unless you're into that kind of thing!), but just lifting heavy objects (your own body weight included) a couple times a week will give you the muscle and definition to be in the best shape of your life. These workouts can be totally sporadic and 30 minutes or less of all out effort. I've outlined some really simple moves you can incorporate into your routine in the section "Fitness Essentials" that I know you'll love!

Catch Me if You Can

Sprinting is the final piece to the Primal fitness puzzle. All it takes is a sprint once a week (or two to three times per month) to create positive and noticeable effects in your fitness plan. By the sheer fact that they are something different, sprints have helped me through dreaded fitness slumps and always spice up my weekly routine. Since I don't do them too often, they've served as my "it's time to switch this up" go-to exercise. Sprinting is seriously amazing at:

- Improving bone density
- Stimulating muscle toning
- Creating fat loss

Depending on your fitness and comfort level, you can start out as basic or advanced. The goal is to sprint with all-out effort for as long as you can—probably anywhere between 10-30 seconds. (Yes, you read that right, I said seconds!) Then, just taper down to a walking or "cool down" pace until you feel ready to sprint again. Beginners may want to start with three or four sprints, while more advanced runners could choose up to six.

No matter how fit you are, you don't need to do too many sprints to get the intended benefit. Of course if you are really athletic, you will do your sprints faster than someone who's out of shape, but you never need to do any more sprint repetitions. If your gym teacher says different, please give them this message from me: "Dude, you're wrong!" Sprint workouts are all about quality, not quantity. Doing

too many can put you in that horrible "chronic exercise" category and totally ruin the intended benefits of the workout. Listen to your body! If you wake up the morning after a sprint workout sore and tired, make a note to self to take it a little easier next time and build the difficulty of your workouts gradually and naturally. I don't care what anyone says—pain is not gain.

Become a Triple Threat

If you want to be really well versed in all things fitness, include these three activities into your extracurricular repertoire:

- Ball Sports: soccer, basketball, softball, and the like improve your hand/eye coordination, keep you thinking on your feet, and provide great cardiovascular activity while being fun.

- Gymnastics: not only is gymnastics great for fitness and flexibility, it's so important for us to constantly work on proprioception. Proprioception (proh-pree-uh-sep-shuhn) is the ability to know where you are in space and time. In other words, if you're upside down doing a flip or cartwheel, proprioception tells you where your hands, arms, feet, etc. need to be in order to complete the move. Having this body awareness also allows you to recover from real life slip-ups like an accidental fall, which helps you avoid injury.

- Water Sports: in addition to getting a great workout, water activity provides resistance and is low low impact on your joints. Not to mention, it's vital to know how to swim and feel comfortable in the water.

Warm-ups, Cool-downs, and Stretching

If you've ever played sports, taken any kind of fitness class, or worked out using an exercise DVD, you have spent time warming-up, cooling-down, and stretching. But is all this necessary? If a bear was chasing down Grokette, do you think she'd ask the bear to hang on a sec while she stretched out her hamstrings? Doubtful. Homegirl RAN! Not only did she run, but she did so effortlessly—with no cramps or pulled muscles afterward.

So what does this have to do with you? Bears certainly aren't chasing you down anytime soon, but can't you just take off in a full sprint like that and not feel any pain while running, or experience sore or tender muscles once you've stopped? Well, that depends on your fitness level, but there's a good chance the answer right now is—you can't. (If that's true, I can help you change this!)

Hang on Mr. Bear, let me stretch...

Most likely, Grokette took a good morning stretch, and an occasional post-nap stretch, with a whole lot of squatting in between. Squatting for Grokette was the natural position for sitting, relaxing, and just hanging out. You know she wasn't sitting in a chair or lounging on the couch like most of us do today. Sitting is actually an unnatural position, especially as much as we do it, and causes more problems than you probably realize, such as:

- Back pain from poor posture.

- Blood clots in legs from slowing blood flow due to long periods of inactivity.

- Muscle atrophy—if you're not using your muscles they will begin to weaken because your body thinks that maintaining inactive muscles is a wasteful use of resources.

- Shortened hip flexors and hamstrings—your body will also adapt by shortening these muscles since sitting requires a shorter "pose" than standing. (If you don't stand much, your body finds it unnecessary to keep your muscles long.)

- Weakened glutes (your booty).

Squatting is a movement you can easily reintroduce into your lifestyle (I say rein-troduce because you used to do it when you were a kid—we all did—that's how natural of a movement it is) with just a little practice. Years of sitting and forcing your body to adapt to bad habits may have you a little out of squat-shape, but we'll get you back in perfect squat form in no time! I've detailed the steps for you in the "Fitness Essentials" section coming up.

Feel like you're not ready to incorporate focused stretching into your daily rou-tine? That's okay! You can simply start by performing smaller versions of your workout to warm up the specific muscle groups you're going to use. For example:

- Sprints: start with an easy walk or light jog.

- Squatting: begin with half-squats, or if you're going to use weights, warm up without them.

- Push-ups: try wall or incline push-ups first to work your way up.

- Pull-ups: consider hanging from the bar for a comfortable amount of time and then slowly lowering yourself back to the ground.

Of course, there are many different activities you'll find yourself partaking in, but based on these examples, you probably have a pretty good idea of how to make modifications to get your muscles ready for the full movement.

If you think you're up for the challenge of adding stretching to your life, the most time I'm going to ask of you is 10 minutes! Seem too good to be true? Well, it's not. Since you're starting young, you don't have years of damage to overcome. You can do a world of good for your muscles, joints, and body in less time than it takes to get ready in the morning!

Stretching Essentials

As promised, I've included my five favorite stretches. These moves have been hand selected just for you and your lifestyle. Make sure to perform them in the order that they appear in the book. These stretches are a progression that will run you through specific muscle groups focused to combat issues you probably face every day: sitting for hours in class, exhibiting poor posture, and wearing high heels or other clunky shoes that may look great but don't feel so good. That means you'll be focusing on your chest, shoulders, back, butt, hips, hamstrings, quadriceps, and calves. For every move, I've explained the area of the body worked, why it needs to be worked, and how to perform the movement.

Run through this progression twice, once for your right side and once for your left. Spend about a minute on each stretch and the entire sequence is about 10 minutes long. Some of these have multiple holds, and depending on your mobility, a few might be a little tougher than others. It's important to listen to your body and NOT to stretch any muscle beyond its limit. Remember, the goal here is to help your body, not harm it. It's also crucial to pay attention to your form. If you can, do these moves in front of a mirror (or any reflective surface like a patio door or a TV with the power off) to be sure your form is correct. Sometimes what feels like the right position isn't actually right at all. You'll want to nail the form the first time so that you're not training your body to move incorrectly or develop bad mobility habits. Consider finding a workout buddy, like a friend or family member. Sometimes a good partner in crime can improve your workout and make it a lot more fun too!

If you ever do "Stretching Essentials" on the same day as "Fitness Essentials" be sure to do the stretches after fitness and not before. These are deep, static stretches that could be a little too intense to perform with cold muscles. Before doing any rigorous stretches or exercises, do some simple dynamic stretching.

The difference between static stretches and dynamic stretches is this: static moves are done when the body is at rest and not in motion, stretching a muscle to its extended range of motion and holding the position for 30 seconds or up to 2 minutes. Dynamic moves are done while in full motion, using momentum to propel your muscles to their extended range of motion. Examples of dynamic stretching that you can implement as a warm-up before any kind of workout include efforts like:

- Leg swings front and back
- Leg swings side to side
- Arm circles forward
- Arm circles backwards
- Walking lunges
- Jumping jacks

If you have any physical limitations or preexisting injuries, you'll want to talk to a parent, gym teacher/coach, or doctor before performing any of the stretches or exercises in this book.

Low Lunge

What

The Low Lunge stretches and improves the mobility of your hip flexors, hamstrings, calves, and quadriceps.

Why

Let's be real for a minute. Even if you wanted to stop sitting so much, odds are you have no choice. Our culture is one that has fully embraced sitting while performing everyday tasks. You're probably sitting while you read this book—bonus points if you aren't! Because of the crazy amount of sitting you do, I'm focusing a lot of your efforts on hip mobility. When you sit too much, your hip flexors tighten and can even shorten over time. This diminishes your range of motion, preventing you from doing something as simple as squatting, and can also cause some serious lower back pain. If you take care of your hips now, you will reap the benefits for the rest of your life.

How

1. Stand with your feet hip width apart and hands on your hips.

2. Go into a lunge by stepping forward with your right foot to the point where your right knee aligns over your right ankle, keeping your right knee at a 90-degree angle. Your shin will be perpendicular to the ground and your thigh will be parallel to the ground. Your left knee will also be bent 90 degrees, with your left shin parallel to the ground and your thigh perpendicular to the ground.

3. Place your left knee on the ground and come off the ball of your foot; lay your left leg flat on the ground. Keep your upper body tall with your shoulders back (don't curl them forward). Sink the hips forward and down. Focus on breathing deeply and at a steady pace; never hold your breath. Hold this position for about a minute.

1 *Stand tall*

2 *Lunge forward*

3 *Sink deep*

Kneeling Hip Stretch

What

The Kneeling Hip Stretch stretches and improves the mobility of your hips and thighs.

Why

Like I explained with the Low Lunge, because of the amount of time you are required to sit, I'm going to make sure you work those hips! As part of your core, your hips contain much of your strength, so it's essential to keep them in tiptop shape.

How

1 Start from the Low Lunge position.

2 With your left hand, carefully lean back to grab your left foot and place your right hand on your right knee. Pull your left foot in towards your body as closely as you can, trying to make your left shin perpendicular to the ground. Be sure not to twist the spine, keep both shoulders facing forward, and do not arch your lower back. Continue breathing, and hold this position for about a minute.

1 *Low lunge* **2** *Raise foot*

Half Split

What

The Half Split stretches and improves the mobility of your calves, hamstrings, and glutes.

Why

In addition to being boy crazy, you're probably starting to become a little shoe crazy too—am I right? While I could sit here and preach about how horrible high heels are for your back, legs, and feet, I'll spare you the lecture (for now) and instead share some stretches that will help you out after a night of teetering on four-inch heels. While heels may help you look taller and lengthen your legs, they're actually doing more damage than you realize. In the name of beauty, you're compromising your posture and damaging joints and muscles…from your shoulders all the way down to your toes. (More on that later!) To counter the destruction to your calf muscles, be sure to stretch them, specifically after nights in your newest sparkly heels.

How

1. Start from the Kneeling Hip Stretch position.

2. Release your left foot back to the ground; keep your toe pointed and leg flat. Shift your weight back and straighten your right leg, with your heel on the ground and your ankle flexed so that your toes point up. Reach to the ground with your fingertips if you are having trouble maintaining your balance.

3. Bend your upper body forward, extending your forehead towards your right ankle. Place your hands flat on the ground (or as close as you can get without straining) and extend your head as low to the ground as you can without bending your right knee. Continue breathing, and hold this position for about a minute.

1 *Hip stretch*   *2* *Shift back*

3 *Bend forward*

Pigeon Pose

What

The Pigeon Pose stretches and improves the mobility of your hip flexors and hip rotator muscles.

Why

You're starting to notice a trend here, huh? Like the Low Lunge and the Kneeling Hip Stretch, I'm sneaking one last hip stretch in here because you likely sit too much.

How

1. Start from the Half Split position.

2. Bring your upper body upright, and shift your weight forward going back to a Low Lunge position.

3. Lower your hands in front of you and shift your right knee onto its right side and extend it forward until it touches your right wrist, keeping your right thigh in line with your body. Slowly pull your right ankle towards you until your right foot is directly below your left hip. Straighten your left leg directly behind you so it's entirely on the ground, and place your right hand on your right knee and your left hand on your right foot.

4. Extend your torso forward, coming down onto your elbows, making sure to keep your hips level. If the stretch feels too intense, come up from the ground as much as you need to and use your arms to support more of your weight. Continue breathing, and hold this position for about a minute.

1 *Half split*

2 *Low lunge*

3 *Tuck leg*

4 *Extend forward*

Tip Over Tuck

What

The Tip Over Tuck stretches and improves the mobility of your chest, shoulders, hamstrings, and lower back.

Why

If you've ever looked at a fashion magazine, watched red carpet coverage, or snooped your favorite celeb's social media page, you've seen it: the slouch. This iconic stance consists of hips thrusted out, lower back arched, hands on hips, and shoulder curled forward. This posture—or lack thereof—became popular back in the 1920s. It served as a form of rebellion; girls back then started listening to jazz music, danced all night, and strayed as far from the "prim and proper" look as they could. While this look was effortlessly cool, it accounts for the poor posture and hunchbacks we see today. The next time you're in class, take a look around. Are most of your classmates at their desks, hunched over with curved backs and shoulders that curl forward? When your back and shoulders lack strength and mobility, you force the curve of your spine to hold your weight up. This can cause all kinds of damage, but you can correct your posture if you're able to get your shoulders back in a natural position.

How

1. Start from the Pigeon Pose position.

2. Bring your body upright, and push yourself up into the Low Lunge position.

3. Stand all the way up on your feet, keeping your feet shoulder width apart. Reach your arms behind you and interlace your fingers.

4. Lean your chest forward and lift your hands up overhead as you fold your torso toward your thighs. Make sure you're lengthening through your spine by reaching the top of your head toward the floor. Continue breathing, and hold this position for about a minute.

1 *Pigeon pose*

2 *Low lunge*

3 *Stand Tall*

4 *Hinge forward*

If this is your first run through Stretching Essentials, go back to the beginning and start the Low Lunge leading with your left foot. If you've just completed both sides, you're done with stretches for the day!

High Heels, High Risk

Remember when I said I would spare you the lecture on wearing heels? Well the time has come…here's the scoop! I will not argue with you—heels make you look amazing and feel like a million bucks, at least for the first 15 minutes. I do wear heels for special occasions, but I'm not like a lot of girls who consider heels a part of their daily ensemble. Why? Well, to be honest, I just can't hang. My little size five-and-a-half feet are aching before I leave the house! Some of my friends assure me that if I just wear heels more often, I'll "break my feet in" and "get used to them," but to be honest, that's the last thing I want. Let's take a closer look at all the damage heels can do to your body:

> • Posture: when your heel is unnaturally higher than your toes, it throws your entire body out of alignment. Your hips, shoulders, back, and spine all suffer.

- Knees: in heels, your body is thrown forward to compensate for balance, putting pressure on your knees. Keep this up and you have arthritis and degenerative joint disease to look forward to when you're older.

- Calf: heels may create the illusion of longer legs, but you're actually forcing your calves to contract. Women who've worn heels all their lives have actually caused their calves to tighten and shorten permanently.

- Achilles Tendon: just like calves, your Achilles tendon can shorten and tighten. If your Achilles tendon is forever shortened, the tendon can become stretched and inflamed. This is known as tendinitis. Your Achilles tendon can even snap, an injury that requires a painful surgery, leaves a massive scar, and takes a long time to heal.

- Heel: ever see a "Pump Bump?" This bump, also known as Haglund's deformity, is a bony enlargement on the back of the heel, and is caused by rubbing and irritation.

- Ankle: with an increased chance of falling in heels, the odds of a sprained or broken ankle are not in your favor.

- Toes: rubbing causes irritation and leads to uncomfortable and unattractive blisters and calluses. Blisters are little pockets of fluid, and calluses develop when the skin hardens and becomes thick and tough.

Fitness Essentials

Now that you have a solid understanding of the Stretching Essentials, what each movement can do for you, and the difference between static and dynamic stretches, let's move on to some fitness moves that will increase your strength. Just like the Stretching Essentials, the Fitness Essentials are to be followed in the order they appear in this book. Depending upon your fitness level, you may wish to run through the circuit two to four (or maybe more) times. However, if this is your first time, once might be enough! Again, everything I stated before in the stretching section applies to fitness. Let's quickly go over those fundamentals again to be sure you don't forget anything.

Warm-up with some dynamic stretches like those listed in Stretching Essentials on page 45. Form is everything! Find a mirror or a buddy to ensure you've got the right form. Don't push beyond your limit, and listen to your body. It knows better than I do about what you can and can't handle. We're all built differently, and just because I can do something or your friend loves a certain move, doesn't mean it will feel the same to you. With that said, if you have any physical limitations or preexisting injuries, talk to a fitness pro before attempting any of the stretches or exercises in this book.

Push-ups

What
Push-ups strengthen your upper/lower body and core.

Why
Push-ups are as close to a perfect workout as you can get—when performed correctly. They work your entire upper body, including your chest, shoulders, and triceps, while also strengthening your lats and traps (which are the large muscle groups in your back). Push-ups use your abs to stabilize and engage your lower back, legs, and glutes—a total body workout! Their awesomeness is often overlooked purely because of how simple they are, but push-ups are truly beneficial to any exercise routine, no matter what your fitness level is.

How
There are three levels of difficulty to push-ups: Wall Push-ups; Incline Push-ups; Floor Push-ups. Choose one that suits your current fitness level, working your way toward the most difficult variation.

Breathing Technique: Inhale each time you lower yourself down towards the wall, bench, or ground, and then exhale on the effort when you push yourself up.

Smarty Pants:

If you've ever seen "modified" push-ups that are performed from the knees as opposed to the toes…that is *not* a push-up! People tend to think push-ups from the knees are a simplified version of the exercise, but the truth is that the bend in your knee disengages almost all of your efforts. Instead, if you're looking for something a little easier, perform your push-ups with the same form against a wall or bench. This will ensure the same muscle groups stay engaged, and you will still reap all the benefits of a traditional floor push-up.

Wall Push-ups (beginner)

1 Stand about one to two feet (or the appropriate distance which allows you to achieve proper form) away from a wall. Place your hands shoulder width apart against the wall. Align your body to be perfectly straight, with core and glutes tight and head facing straight ahead, and then go up onto your toes.

2 Keep your body in perfect alignment (don't push your butt out or sag your hips down), and lower your upper body towards the wall, bending at the elbows and keeping the arms in tight next to the body—don't let them fly out to the sides. Then come back up to starting position. That counts as one repetition (rep); do as many reps as you can for one minute while maintaining proper form. Movements should be slow and controlled.

1 *On wall*   **2** *Lower yourself*

Incline Push-ups (moderate)

1 Stand about one to two feet (or the appropriate distance which allows you to achieve proper form) away from a sturdy bench or other object elevated from the ground. Assume the same position previously mentioned: body perfectly straight, core and glutes tight, head facing straight ahead, and go up onto your toes.

2 Keep your body in perfect alignment, and lower your upper body towards the bench, bending at the elbows and keeping the arms in tight next to the body—don't let them fly out to the sides. Then come back up to starting position. That counts as one rep; do as many reps as you can for one minute while maintaining proper form. Movements should be slow and controlled.

1 On bench

2 Lower yourself

Floor Push-ups (advanced)

1. Starting from the floor, assume the same position previously mentioned: body perfectly aligned, core and glutes tight, head facing straight ahead, go up onto your toes and on your hands.

2. Keep your body in perfect alignment, and lower your upper body towards the ground, bending at the elbows and keeping the arms in tight next to the body—don't let them fly out to the sides. Then come back up to starting position. That counts as one rep; do as many reps as you can for one minute while maintaining proper form. Movements should be slow and controlled.

1 *On floor*

2 *Lower yourself*

Squats

What
Squats strengthen your lower body, glutes, and core.

Why
Not only will squatting strengthen your core and lower body, but it will also improve your mobility. If you're having trouble squatting properly, it's likely due to shortened hip flexors and hamstrings from sitting too much. Think back to all the hip flexor and hamstring stretches you did in the previous section—this is where those stretches will pay off.

How
There are three levels of difficulty to squats: Assisted Squats; Half Squats; Full Squats. Choose one that suits your current fitness level, working your way toward the most difficult variation.

Breathing Technique: Inhale each time you lower yourself down towards the ground, and then exhale on the effort when you push yourself up.

Assisted Squats (beginner)

1 Stand tall about a foot (or the appropriate distance which allows you to achieve proper form) away from a sturdy pole or support object and grab ahold of it. Place feet shoulder width apart, with toes pointed forward or naturally pointed out slightly.

2 Keep your core tight and your chest tall. Sit back by hinging at your hips, lowering yourself between your knees by extending your butt out and bringing your thighs parallel or below parallel to the ground. Pause momentarily, then return to a standing position, squeezing your butt on the way up. Make sure your knees stay in line with your feet. That counts as one rep; do as many reps as you can for one minute while maintaining proper form. Movements should be slow and controlled.

1 *Hang on*

2 *Squat deep*

Half Squats (moderate)

1. Assume the same position previously mentioned: feet shoulder width apart, with toes pointed forward or naturally pointed out slightly. Extend arms straight out in front of you for balance.

2. Keep your core tight and your chest tall. Sit back by hinging at your hips, lowering yourself between your knees by extending your butt out and bringing your thighs above parallel with the ground, about 45 degrees. Pause momentarily, then return to a standing position, squeezing your butt on the way up. Make sure your knees stay in line with your feet. That counts as one rep; do as many reps as you can for one minute while maintaining proper form. Movements should be slow and controlled.

1 *Arms out*

2 *Squat shallow*

Full Squats (advanced)

1 Assume the same position previously mentioned: feet shoulder width apart, with toes pointed forward or naturally pointed out slightly. Extend arms straight out in front of you for balance.

2 Keep your core tight and your chest tall. Sit back by hinging at your hips, lowering yourself between your knees by extending your butt out and bringing your thighs parallel or below parallel to the ground. Pause momentarily, then return to a standing position, squeezing your butt on the way up. Make sure your knees stay in line with your feet. That counts as one rep; do as many reps as you can for one minute while maintaining proper form. Movements should be slow and controlled.

1 *Arms out*   **2** *Squat deep*

Pull-ups

What
Pull-ups strengthen your upper body, back, and core.

Why
Anytime you do an exercise that makes you "push" (like push-ups), you need to counter that effort with a move that makes you "pull" (like pull-ups). And just like push-ups, pull-ups engage your entire upper body, especially the muscles in your back, as well as your abs and biceps.

How
There are three levels of difficulty to pull-ups: Chin Hold; Chin-ups; Pull-ups. Choose one that suits your current fitness level, working your way toward the most difficult variation.

Breathing Technique: Inhale each time you slowly lower yourself down from the bar, and then exhale on the effort when you pull yourself up. If doing a chin hold, breathe deeply at a steady pace and never hold your breath.

Chin Hold (beginner)

1 Place a sturdy chair beneath a pull-up bar. Step up onto the chair and hold the bar with your palms facing towards you, shoulder width apart.

2 Secure your chin above the bar. Keep your elbows tight, grip the bar, and pull your legs off the chair. (Let them hang or cross your feet at the ankles.) Hang from the bar in this position as long as you can, then slowly lower yourself back toward the ground. This part is crucial, as it will help you build strength.

1 *Grip bar*

2 *Hang tight*

Chin-ups (moderate)

1. Hang (legs straight down or crossed at the ankles) beneath a pull-up bar, and hold the bar with your palms facing towards you, shoulder width apart.

2. Keep your elbows tight, chin tucked, and shoulder blades retracted to protect the spine. Lead with the chest and raise your chin over the bar. Gradually lower all the way back down to starting position. That counts as one rep; do as many reps as you can while maintaining proper form. Movements should be slow and controlled.

1. *Under Grip*

2. *Raise up*

Pull-ups (advanced)

1. Hang (legs straight down or crossed at the ankles) beneath a pull-up bar, and hold the bar with your palms facing away from you, shoulder width apart.

2. Keep your elbows tight, chin tucked, and shoulder blades retracted to protect the spine. Lead with the chest and raise your chin over the bar. Gradually lower all the way back down to starting position. That counts as one rep; do as many reps as you can while maintaining proper form. Movements should be slow and controlled.

1 Over grip *2 Raise up*

Lunges

What
Lunges strengthen your lower body, glutes, and core

Why
Similar to squats, lunges work your hips and force you to find balance. Performing moves that engage your balance encourages you to tighten large muscle groups and focus on stability.

How
There are two versions of lunges: Forward Lunge; Reverse Lunge. They are the same level of difficulty when it comes to strength, although some people find forward lunges easier than reverse lunges when it comes to balance. Since they work different muscle groups, work on technique for both.

Breathing Technique: Inhale each time you lower yourself down towards the ground, and then exhale on the effort when you push yourself up.

Forward Lunges (better for the quadriceps)

1 Stand with your feet hip width apart and your hands on your hips.

2 Go into a lunge by stepping forward with your right foot three to four feet. Bend your right knee 90 degrees, keeping it directly above your right ankle. Be careful to never let your knee pass your ankle; it could strain your knee and cause injury. Your shin will be perpendicular to the ground with your thigh parallel to the ground. Your left knee will also be bent 90 degrees, with your left shin parallel to the ground and your thigh perpendicular to the ground. Spring back to starting position by returning your right foot next to your left foot. Then repeat this move leading with your left foot. Both moves together count as one rep; do as many reps as you can for one minute while maintaining proper form. Movements should be slow and controlled.

1 *Stand tall*

2 *Lunge forward*

Reverse Lunges (better for the glutes)

1 Stand with your feet hip width apart and your hands on your hips.

2 Go into a reverse lunge by stepping backwards with your right foot three to four feet. Bend your right knee 90 degrees, with your right shin parallel to the ground and your thigh perpendicular to the ground. Your left knee will also be bent 90 degrees, with your left shin perpendicular to the ground and your thigh parallel to the ground. Be sure to keep your left knee in alignment directly above your left ankle. Spring back to starting position by returning your right foot next to your left foot. Then repeat this move leading with your left foot. Both moves together count as one rep; do as many reps as you can for one minute while maintaining proper form. Movements should be slow and controlled.

1 *Stand tall*

2 *Lunge backwards*

Plank

What
The plank strengthens your upper/lower body and core.

Why
Performing a plank engages your entire body. Don't let this move fool you—it's tougher than it looks. Just clear your mind, focus on your breathing, and you will master this move in no time.

How
There are two levels of difficulty to the plank: Forearm Plank; Hand Plank. Choose one that suits your current fitness level, working your way toward the most difficult variation.

Breathing Technique: Breathe deeply at a steady pace and never hold your breath.

Forearm Plank (beginner)

1 Starting from your knees, place your elbows on the ground, aligned directly beneath your shoulders. Keep hands flat on the floor in front of you, or cup hands for a bit more stability.

2 Extend your legs behind you, and rise onto your toes with the body perfectly horizontal (don't push your butt out or sag your hips down). Continue to breathe and hold this position as long as you can up to one minute while maintaining proper form.

1 *Elbows down* **2** *Align body*

Hand Plank (advanced)

1 Starting from your knees, place your hands on the ground, aligned directly beneath your shoulders.

2 Extend your legs behind you, and rise onto your toes with the body perfectly horizontal. Continue to breathe and hold this position as long as you can up to one minute while maintaining proper form.

1 *Hand down*

2 *Align body*

If this is your first run through Fitness Essentials, go back to the beginning and start another circuit until you've done the appropriate amount of sets for your fitness level. If you've just completed all of your sets, you're done with fitness for the day!

What Is Primal Fitness

Primal fitness ditches conventional wisdom's love of chronic cardio, and instead encourages you to focus on three simple fitness principles: move everyday, lift heavy things, and sprint once a week.

Move Everyday

It's time to get off the couch and start moving. There are a lot of easy ways to include movement into your everyday life, like walking to and from school. A simple way to keep track of movement goals is to download an app and set goals for your time, distance, or even speed. Remember, the goal is two to five hours per week.

Do You Even Lift, Bro?

Lifting heavy things will not make you bulky. Instead it builds lean muscle, making you stronger and more fit. Heavy weights include your own body weight, and strengthening exercises only need to last 30 minutes at most a couple times per week.

Catch Me if You Can

Sprinting workouts are the shortest workouts you will perform, sometimes lasting as little as five minutes. Your goal is once a week, but two to three times per month is good enough if you're keeping up with moving and lifting heavy things. Not only are sprints great for your body, but they can also help you bust through annoying weight loss or fitness plateaus.

Warm-ups, Cool-downs, and Stretching

Our ancestors may not have needed to stretch before physical activity, but they were naturally in optimal physical health. Since you likely are not in the same shape they were in, it's beneficial to your muscles, bones, and joints to warm up and stretch before and/or after physical activity.

Stretching Essentials

The five Stretching Essentials include: Low Lunge, Kneeling Hip Stretch, Half Split, Pigeon Pose, and Tip Over Tuck. This progression of stretches has a big focus on your hips, and also target your core, upper, and lower body.

High Heels, High Risk

High heels might make you look amazing for the night, but they can cause real damage to your body over time affecting your posture, knees, calves, Achilles tendon, heels, ankles, and toes. Ouch!

Fitness Essentials

The five Fitness Essentials are Push-ups, Squats, Pull-ups, Lunges, and Plank. Together, these moves cover a full body workout, focusing on upper/lower body, core, stability, and balance. Every stretch and exercise can be accomplished without the use of any equipment or weights, and you are encouraged to speak to a parent, gym teacher/coach, or doctor if you have any questions, physical limitations, or preexisting injuries.

Chapter Three

Life 101: The Other Important Stuff

Catching Quality Zzzs

Ah yes, sleep. I love sleep. You love sleep. Who doesn't love sleep? Snoozing is not only an enjoyable thing to do, but it's also a time for your body and mind to heal and restore your energy after a busy day. Getting enough sleep every night (yes, naps count too) has been proven to:

- Increase alertness
- Boost creativity
- Lower stress
- Promote fat loss and a healthy weight
- Elevate mood
- Improve memory
- Enhance muscle repair

The importance of sleep, especially napping, is pretty much ignored in our hectic, technology-obsessed world. We are so consumed with busy schedules, high-tech gadgets and constant, in-your-face entertainment that we tend to forget about rest. I know I've felt guilty in the past for napping—feeling as if I'm being irresponsible, lazy, or wasting my time, but this couldn't be further from the truth. When you feel tired, there is nothing more important than getting some rest. That's right, not even homework, a big final exam, or your friends' buzzing text messages should have a higher priority than resting and recharging. If you try to "push through" those times when you're tired, you not only think less effectively, but you also affect your health in many ways.

Ten thousand years ago, your ancestors were on a schedule with the sun. They woke up naturally and full of energy, right around sunrise. After the sun set, life slowed down big time. Have you ever been camping? There's not a whole heck of a lot to do after it gets dark. Maybe you tell a few ghost stories by the campfire, then pretty soon someone yawns and everyone passes out.

What this means is that most everything you do after the sun goes down isn't Primal, especially when what you're doing has a screen that emits light. Can you think of anything that qualifies? How about a TV, computer, or cell phone? Now, using digital distractions isn't Primal during the day either, but engaging with super bright screens at night does way more damage. Your body simply is not accustomed to artificial light sources after the sun sets; expose yourself to these bright lights, and you can seriously mess up your health.

I hope she doesn't burn her hand.

Ok, I know you're scratching your head wondering how in the world something like watching TV at night can be harmful to your health, so let me explain. For starters, when you're exposed to the stimulation of a bright screen at night, it keeps you awake longer than you're evolutionarily designed to be. I don't mean just the time spent on the couch watching your favorite reality show; I'm including the time it takes to decompress after the TV is turned off. The glow from that flat screen actually suppresses your body's production of melatonin, the chemical that helps you sleep. Not only that, but while your melatonin is dwindling, your cortisol (the stress hormone that makes you crave sugar and store fat) is skyrocketing. Ever wonder why you get the late night munchies while you're crashed out on the couch? Well, now you know why.

When you were a kid, your circadian rhythm, or internal clock, probably sent signals to your brain that you were ready for bed around 8 or 9 pm. Sound about right? Well, once you hit your teen years, this clock goes through a bit of a reset. Melatonin actually starts to release later at night in the brain of a teen than it does in that of an adult or little kid. Like you needed more reasons to cut out the glowing stimuli of TV, computers, tablets, and cell phones!

And how about the cruel timing this circadian rhythm reboot has on your life...right when you have to deal with early school hours, an overload of homework and tests, sports obligations, maybe you just got a part-time job...and let's not forget your ever growing social life. How are you supposed to take care of all your responsibilities and get enough hours of sleep each night?

For most of us, "enough sleep" means between eight and a half and nine hours of sleep each night. How do you fit into this average? Most teens only catch between six and seven hours of zzzs per night. Does that sound a little more like your sleep schedule?

Some of your friends or other people at school might take pills or drink energy drinks to "make up" for the sleep they've missed. That stuff is gross, and there is nothing in a bottle that can magically replace good quality sleep. Artificial stimulants are only causing more damage and I highly suggest not using them.

If you're looking for ways to balance sleep and, well, life, let me recommend some possible solutions to help you sneak in some extra shut-eye…even if it's only 15 or 30 extra minutes, because every second makes a difference!

- Try taking baths or showers at night: spending a little time soaking might help you relax and will definitely save you time in the morning.

- Don't procrastinate: take care of any homework or chores/errands that you have earlier in the day. If you put them off until 10 pm you could be stuck with an unplanned all-nighter.

- Pencil it in: you have schedules for classes, sports, work, and your social life, why not pencil in sleep and nap time? Become a master planner!

- Stay active when the sun's up: if you use up all of your energy during the day, your body will likely accept sleep at night.

- Keep an empty tank: avoid eating within two hours of bedtime, and certainly stay away from caffeine drinks for at least eight hours before bedtime. (Yup—the effects can last that long or even longer!) Bonus: an empty stomach at bedtime translates into better fat burning while you sleep! Who's going to argue with that?

- Create a dreamy cave: if your bedroom is a cluttered mess, too warm, and full of light (perhaps from a street light or city lights shining in through curtains or blinds), it's time for a massive makeover!

  - Eliminate piles of clothes, junk, and schoolwork.

  - Make your room cool—68 degrees Fahrenheit is supposed to be the ideal sleeping temperature. Use a fan to cool things down if you need to.

  - Make your room completely dark. If you have curtains that don't block light, get some blackout curtains. They're pretty cheap and super easy to install.

  - Ditch the mermaid night-light that you got for your sixth birthday. There is a strict "zero light" policy when it's time to sleep.

  - If your environment is noisy, consider a pair of earplugs—just be sure you've got a game plan to hear the alarm clock in the morning!

  - Speaking of alarm clocks, it would be ideal if you didn't even need one. Hopefully when you have good Primal habits in the evening—after mellowing out on the screen use—you will wake up naturally refreshed and energized in the morning, soon after sunrise. When you wake up with the sun, it helps trigger the right flow of hormones to give you energy naturally. You won't need Starbucks in the morning if you back off your computer in the evening!

- Don't overthink it: if you often have a hard time falling asleep at night, just the act of worrying about falling asleep can keep you awake. If you find yourself wide-eyed after 15 or 20 minutes of lying down, try reading a book, making a list of the thoughts racing through your mind (hey, if they're on paper they don't need to be in your head), or doing something else low-key until your body signals it's ready for sleep. Sorry—videogames, TV, and social media are not considered low-key activities.

Let's face it, when your brain is tired, you will fall asleep (or at least zone out) no matter what you're doing. So the next time you feel like you have to stay up late and study for an important test, realize that you're better off giving your brain some rest. Your late night study session and lack of good night's sleep will cause your brain to totally space out instead of focusing when the test is in front of you.

Never Stop Playing

No really, never stop playing. It's awesome. I understand it's easy to feel like you're getting too old to play because you're too busy with school, sports, or just "trying to be cool," but play really is one of the easiest ways to stay fit, strong, and happy. Maybe you just don't like the word "play" because it sounds like something a baby does? Okay, let me rename it for you—let's call it "adventure."

Partaking in super sophisticated teen adventures is a great thing to do now (and until you're old and gray) because play—oops, I mean adventure—will help your mind and body in many ways, including:

- Increase strength, endurance, flexibility, and balance
- Enhance creativity
- Fine-tune your social skills
- Boost your sense of humor
- Give you a better sense of freedom and independence
- Increase self-confidence
- Relieve stress
- Enhance your teamwork ability
- Improve your overall quality of life
- And don't forget that it's fun!

The most excellent part of playing (eh, just deal with it, I'm calling it playing!) is that there are no rules. When you were a child, no one dumped a bunch of rules on you, blew whistles in your face, or criticized your technique when you were playing, and it won't happen now either. Play is all about following your heart, your creativity, and your desire to be active. You'll know you're doing it right when you find yourself completely lost in the moment.

The same goes for our ancestors. Even though Grokette had a really difficult life full of hard work, anthropologists are certain that she played regularly. Our ancestors realized that they needed ways to unwind and de-stress from the grind and the danger of daily life. They engaged in all kinds of play that served as entertainment and a way to strengthen social bonding and learn new skills. If you watch puppies in action, or even wild animals like wolves or lions, you'll see young cubs roughhousing with each other all day long. Of course, they aren't trying to hurt their siblings; they are actually honing their hunting skills for when it's time to move from play to reality!

The beauty of play, unlike sports or other organized activities, is that there are no strict guidelines and no demands on your time. Here are some of my favorite ways to play and get the most out of life:

- Walking my dogs: there are few things I love more than my two Boston Terriers (they're actually laying at my feet as I type these words). They fill my life with so much joy and I like to return the favor by taking them for walks every evening. (They *love* walks.) I even incorporate my weekly sprint sessions into these dog walks because it's exciting for them and it's just way more fun to run with a partner or two...even if those partners are furry and run with their tongues out!

- Monkeying around: I live close to the famous Muscle Beach in Venice, California, and it's one of my favorite spots to play. I really love doing flips or hanging upside down on the parallel bars, soaring through the air on the giant swing sets, and flying around like a monkey on the rings. It's a killer workout, but I barely realize it because I'm having way too much fun to even notice!

- Mountain climber: because of where I live, I'm also lucky enough to be within driving distance to some really incredible mountain trails. One of my favorite sites to climb is Stony Point in the San Fernando Valley. The landscape is a blend of hiking paths and rock climbing spots. It's a great chance to explore, use problem-solving to navigate tricky terrain, and experience a breathtaking view when you reach the top! Talk about some serious payoff.

- Dolphin taxi: at this point you've probably gathered that I like to take advantage of the incredible environment I live in. While I do live very close to the beach, I'm kind of a wimp and think the water of the Pacific Ocean is too cold (even in the summer months). I do, however, love playing in the ocean. Last year I spent a couple weeks in Playa Del Carmen, Mexico where the water is crystal clear and super warm. I could spend my entire day jumping and swimming in those waves. It's a great workout and boy, does it keep you alert. Timing waves with jumps and dives, or hoping on a friend's back is serious business. It takes a lot of planning, problem solving, and agility!

And these are just the things I like to do to take advantage of the beautiful state that I live in. You don't need to live next to the ocean or near any mountains to go on your own adventure. Explore the place you're from and see what kinds of exciting journeys you can find.

Fun in the Sun

By nature, you were meant to spend a lot of time in the sun. Our planet clearly did not come equipped with houses, skyscrapers, or shopping centers, which means our ancestors spent the majority of their time in the great outdoors. Sure, they built primitive homes or took refuge in caves (insert cheesy caveman joke here) when they had access to them, but they were very comfortable with being outside, and actually thrived in their environments.

Spending some quality time in the sun not only improves your mood and gives your skin some healthy color, but it also supplies your body with a good dose of vitamin D. This awesome vitamin (it's technically a hormone, but everyone calls it a "vitamin") has recently been referred to as the new "wonder vitamin" as experts continue to learn about its role in healthy lifestyles and disease prevention. Vitamin D is essential for:

- Healthy bones, teeth, and nails
- Good eyesight
- The absorption of other key vitamins like A and C, and calcium
- Boosting your immune system
- Lowering the chances of developing heart disease, certain cancers, diabetes, and inflammatory conditions

Sadly most people, including teenagers, don't get enough vitamin D. We tend to spend too much time indoors and lack proper nutrition through diet alone. So how much sun should you get? Depending on your complexion, anywhere between 10 and 30 minutes every day should be enough to get a good dose. You need to expose large skin surface areas of your body to the sun. Since your face typically gets more exposure than any other part of your body (and is also the most sensitive skin), give it a break by wearing a hat and sunglasses or sitting in partial shade and exposing as many other parts of your body to the sun as you can.

Of course, like everything else, moderation is key. If you're lathering up with oil and spending hours in the sun, you could be absorbing too many harmful UVA and UVB rays. These harmful rays can sometimes cause melanoma, which is a type of skin cancer. If you've ever had sunburn, it means you got too much sun. The best guideline is to never burn, but to try and maintain a slight tan during the months of the year when the sun shines the brightest. If you choose to protect your skin with sunscreen, avoid products that contain oxybenzone— a chemical that's been shown to "disrupt hormonal function." Creepy! Instead, try covering up with protective clothing or use all-natural sunblocks that feature zinc oxide (the safest and most effective UV-filter) as the active ingredient.

In addition to sunshine, you can also get vitamin D from foods like eggs, fatty fish, and fish oils such as salmon, mackerel, and cod liver oil. All of these foods are 100 percent paleo and you've probably already been working them into your diet, haven't you? Oh, I'm so proud!

Learn to love the sun...but not too much!

Use That Noggin

That may be common sense…or is it? Our ancestors were smart, and they had to be—it meant the difference between life and death! This modern world entails far fewer risks than those that faced our ancestors 10,000 years ago, but our lapses in judgement make us more susceptible to dangerous accidents. The truth is, the margin of error was much smaller back then. Think about it—but don't hurt yourself!

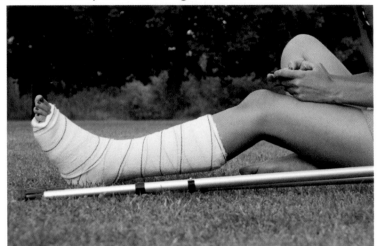

Let's consider a worst-case scenario, here. Imagine you fell while hiking in the woods and broke your leg. Whoops. That's going to suck no matter what time period you live in—but let's examine the aftermath.

You Broke Your Leg Today

- Wham! Yup, that's broken. Your BFF grabs her cell and calls 911 (that is after posting a picture of you screaming in pain online, of course…57 likes!)
- Paramedics arrive in minutes, put you in the ambulance, and speed you off to the hospital.
- X-ray shows you really did a number on that tibia (your shinbone).
- The doctor sets your broken bone, puts your leg in a cast, and tells you to stay off it for three months while it heals.
- During that time, you hang out in bed, watch TV, sleep A LOT, socialize with your friends online, get spoiled by Mom, and pretty much live like a queen.
- Three months later, the Doc is pleased with how much you've healed and takes the cast off.
- You impress everyone at school with your dramatic story of how you almost died a few months ago, but you're pretty sure you have super hero powers that saved you.

Now let's take a look at how this chain of events would have played out if you made a mistake like this 10,000 years ago…

You Broke Your Leg 10,000 Years Ago

- Wham! Yup, that's broken. Your BFF runs five miles back to the tribe to get help.
- After two agonizing hours alone, your friend, along with some adults, arrives to carry you back to the village. Boy is that a bumpy and painful trek home.
- No one can tell exactly what's wrong or if it's actually broken; all of the injuries are internal.
- Dad wraps some hide around your leg and hopes you feel better soon.
- In that time you are lying on the ground in the shade, in A LOT of pain, your Mom has to spend more time gathering food since you can't help her, causing her to become overworked, and you pretty much hate life.
- A mountain lion comes into your village.
- He eats you for dinner.

I bet you didn't see that plot twist coming! Okay, I know that's kind of a silly story, but the moral is this: your constant protection from danger often desensitizes you from its real existence. Let me explain further. Today, a lot of people have a very reckless sense of invincibility. Teens especially think that nothing can hurt them and that if there is ever a problem, someone or something can save them. In this scenario, the doctors used medical technology to fix your leg and your parents used the conveniences of modern life to keep you safe and comfortable.

Before technology and the conveniences of the modern world, teens had to be savvy. They knew that they weren't untouchable, so they stayed sharp, thought critically, and used a lot of common sense to stay out of trouble.

Aww, but he's such a cute kitty...

You don't have to worry about mountain lions anytime soon, and that's great, but let's consider the top three causes of teen deaths today.

- 48 percent is from unintentional mishaps. (73 percent of mishaps are car accidents—don't text and drive!)
- 13 percent is from homicide (murder).
- 11 percent is from suicide.

Umm, hello…that's pretty messed up! We've worked so hard for thousands of years to progress our society. To become smarter, safer, and more secure, and yet today we still make stupid mistakes that lead to the same sad ending as getting eaten by a mountain lion. So let's be smart. Let's be safe, love each other, and love ourselves.

With this understanding, how can you be a savvy Primal teen in this modern world? You could simply start by doing things that stimulate your brain. Your ancestors learned a lot about problem solving, interacting, critical thinking, creativity, and common sense through the actions of their everyday lives. Your generation is bombarded with sensory overload, causing you to think less, become restless, underutilized, and unfulfilled.

You could consider using technology to your advantage. Instead of spending hours online mindlessly interacting with pseudo-friends, watching stupid videos, and looking at pictures of cats, you could use that time to learn something. Or better yet, what if you turned your computer off and read a book? (Oh look, you're already doing that—good for you!) Or spent time with your family? Or established a new hobby? The more you enrich your brain with new information, explore different thoughts and feelings, and experience all the world has to offer, the more amazing and dynamic you will become.

Stay Ahead of the Pack!

Let's take a minute now to peer into your future. When you picture yourself 10, 20, or even 30 years from now, what do you see? Are you lean, healthy, and full of energy? Or are you overweight, out of shape, and on a lot of medication? If you're anything like me, you want the healthy future.

Did you know that the way you eat and how active you are in your teens determines the type of adult you become? Don't put your health off! The longer you stay on a path of junk food and inactivity, the longer it will take to break those bad habits and reverse the damage you've done. Ask any adult you know; I promise they'll tell you to start early…and they say this from experience!

Unhealthy adults who decide to fight back and take the fate of their health into their own hands can spend months, or even years, trying to reclaim the weight

loss, health, and energy they experienced in their teens. If you follow the advice in this book, you won't have to waste all that time working your butt off (literally) to get back something you already have! Even if you're a little overweight as a teen, it's so much easier to get your lifestyle in control now before you become accustomed to unhealthy choices that may just stick with you when you're an adult.

In addition to setting yourself up for a healthy future, you're also allowing yourself to function at optimal health now. This will keep you sharper in class, quicker on the court, and happier in your social life.

Chapter Three: At a Glance

Catching Quality Zzzs
The average teen requires between eight and a half and nine hours of sleep each night, but most only get around six or seven hours. A lot of this has to do with post-daylight exposure, causing a shift in your circadian rhythm, or internal alarm clock. There are some tricks you can implement, like taking a bath before bed, which can sometimes help you get a good night's sleep.

Never Stop Playing
Playing is good for you because it enhances your creativity, gives you a sense of freedom and independence, and relieves stress, just to name a few of the benefits. You should never stop playing, because play just might be the true fountain of youth!

Fun in the Sun
Between 10 and 30 minutes of sun every day can help you get the adequate amount of vitamin D your body requires. Too much sun can expose you to unhealthy levels of UVA and UVB rays that can cause melanoma, which is a type of skin cancer. If you must be in the sun for prolonged periods, consider covering up with protective clothing or use all-natural sunblocks that feature zinc oxide as the active ingredient. Avoid suncreens that use oxybenzone.

Use That Noggin
The conveniences of the modern world may have made your bright and sharp mind dull and unchallenged. Don't fall victim to mind-numbing over stimulus of your everyday life, and instead fight back and become someone extraordinary. Expand your horizons and always push to better your mind, body, and spirit.

Stay Ahead of the Pack!
Starting on your Primal journey now at such a young age will not only help you become a healthy adult, but will also make you one heck of a teen. With optimal health, you will look and feel better than your peers who aren't looking out for their best interests. Put your health first and you'll reap the benefits for the rest of your life!

Chapter Four

Puberty 101: The Down and Dirty

What Is Puberty?

Probably one of the more awkward topics to discuss in class with a bunch of your friends and other students is puberty. Puberty is the physical maturation of your body's sex characteristics: when boys start looking, talking, and acting more like men, and when girls start looking, talking, and acting more like women. Any topic remotely related to the subject of puberty can easily be embarrassing in certain settings. Sure, you're old enough now that you don't giggle at the word "butt," however, things like "breast development" or "body odor" can be tough to talk about when you're self-conscious about these issues in the first place.

So let's dive into the topic of puberty in the privacy of your own home! Maybe after you have a better understanding of the topic and what to expect, it won't feel so silly to discuss around your friends, parents, or teachers.

Puberty is a very different process for guys and girls. We're obviously going to focus on girls in this book, but I do want to touch briefly on what boys go through so that they don't seem as crazy to you. You're all on this wild roller coaster ride together.

For girls, the first signs of puberty usually begin any time between the ages of 7 and 14. Between the ages of 15 and 17, the accelerated physical development typically ends. This means you have grown to your full height (some doctors state that you will stop growing about two years after your first period), your hormone levels settle down, and you are technically a physically mature woman. While you probably associate getting your period with starting puberty, this isn't actually the first step in the process. Let's go through some of the stages of development to better understand what the heck is going on with your body inside and out.

Pancakes, Anyone?

Just when you thought your first time talking about puberty in school was awkward, let's talk about my first experience. I was in fourth grade, and girls and boys were separated into two different rooms to watch a video about puberty for their particular sex. The video was so old and cheesy that my friends and I started making fun of it. The worst part of the video was a scene from a slumber party. Little Janie

got her very first period and the girls asked the Mom all kinds of questions about what a period was and why girls get them. The Mom was in the middle of cooking breakfast for the girls and drew a diagram of a uterus, ovaries, and fallopian tubes with pancake batter. Reproductive organ pancakes, anyone? We all started cracking up and my friends turned to me and said, "Your mom would *so* do that!" My mom was our Girl Scout leader at the time and I was absolutely humiliated!

I obviously survived the embarrassing situation and it's actually one of my favorite "sex ed" stories to tell. But here's my point—a lot of kids are nervous or insecure about the topic of puberty; however, it's just a normal part of growing up and I swear it's not as bad as it seems. And the best part is, you'll get to laugh about these stories when you're older!

Please step away from the pancakes...

Hormones Galore

All right, let's get *sciency* for a minute! I'm going to take you on a trip through the first few events that set this puberty rollercoaster into motion. When your brain decides you're ready, it releases what's called the gonadotropin-releasing hormone (pronounced goh-nad-uh-troh-pin), or we can just call it GnRH for short. This magical hormone takes a little ride through your brain to your pituitary gland (a tiny pea-shaped gland just under your brain), where it releases two puberty hormones: luteinizing hormone (LH) and follicle-stimulating hormone (FSH). Once LH and FSH are swimming around in your bloodstream, they go to work on your ovaries to help produce one final and very important hormone called estrogen. These three hormones work together to help the female body mature and essentially prepare for pregnancy. You follow? Basically one day your brain says, "Okay, let's do this," and then a bunch of hormones are released and your puberty development is set into motion.

This whole process occurs for one reason: to prepare you for pregnancy. I know, it's crazy to think about baby-making when you're still a teenager, but physically and genetically speaking, it's the primary purpose of your physical body. Now, it's important to understand that just because your body is wired to have babies doesn't mean you ever have to get pregnant. Today, we have increased acceptance for those who simply don't choose the traditional path of getting married and having kids. Adult women have more power and freedom than women living in the old days, when society kind of just expected them to get married, crank out some babies, and serve their husband. No thank you! Today, many women who choose not to have children and/or not even get married live long, happy, healthy, productive lives. Anyway, deciding whether to have a baby someday is a discussion for another time, but it's important to understand the biological reason for the hormonal happenings in your body during puberty.

Upstairs/Downstairs

The first physical changes you will notice are the development of your breasts and the growth of pubic hair around your vagina. It's called pubic hair because the skeletal bone in that area is called the pubic bone. In most girls, breast development begins first. However, 15 percent of girls discover their first pubic hairs before seeing any changes "upstairs." Either order is normal, so don't stress!

Breast Development
- Stage 1: no breast tissue present.
- Stage 2: the "breast bud" stage when breast tissue begins to develop, the areola (or the circle of color in the center of your breast) starts to grow wider, and the nipple (or the center of the areola) begins to rise.
- Stage 3: further enlargement of breast tissues and the areola.
- Stage 4: the areola and nipple start to protrude from the breast mound, creating separate "layers."
- Stage 5: mature stage; when the nipple grows fully out.

Pubic Hair Development
- Stage 1: no pubic hair present.
- Stage 2: some sparse hair growth begins around the labia (or the externally visible portion of the vagina). These hairs are straight or curly, and slightly darker than the rest of your body hair.
- Stage 3: hair that is darker, coarser, and curlier continues to grow and spread across the pubic mound, or the pubic bone area.
- Stage 4: hair growth becomes denser and continues to fill in the "pubic triangle" area of the pubic mound.
- Stage 5: pubic hair begins to spread to the thighs and sometimes upwards towards the belly button.

That Time of the Month

As I mentioned earlier, getting your first period isn't the start of puberty. If you've experienced your period, you're already at least two to two and a half years into the process. While most girls understand that having your period means that you are now fertile, or physically able to have children, not everyone understands exactly what your period is, where it comes from, and why you have it.

Your first period—called menarche (pronounced meh-nar-kee)—doesn't occur until all the parts of your reproductive system have fully matured and are able to work together. Those parts include the ovaries, fallopian tubes, and uterus. The ovaries are oval-shaped and are located on each side of the uterus. Inside each girl's ovaries are about 400,000 follicles or potential eggs (that are about 1/10th the size of a poppy seed), all of which are developed before you are born. So, if you want to get super technical, when your Mom was pregnant with you, she also had her future grandchildren in her belly—what a crazy thought!

Getting back to those 400,000 potential eggs, your ovaries release one every menstrual cycle. These releases occur about once a month, and the right and left ovaries take turns releasing eggs. Don't worry, just because you have 400,000 of them, doesn't mean you have to put up with 400,000 periods in your lifetime! Only several hundred of these "eggs" will actually be released during your reproductive years.

After a potential egg is released, it travels down a fallopian tube—a long and thin tube connecting your ovaries to your uterus—towards the uterus, which is located in the lower part of the pelvis. This process is called ovulation. A couple days before ovulation takes place, a hormone called estrogen keeps your uterus (or womb) busy telling it to prepare for a potential baby. During this prep time, your uterus starts to build up its lining with extra blood and tissue. This padded wall makes a comfy place for a baby to begin its development. If by chance the egg becomes fertilized (by a male's sperm, through sexual intercourse), it will make itself right at home in your uterus, attaching to the cozy walls where the magic of life takes place in less than a year!

If the egg doesn't become fertilized, it will not attach to the wall of the uterus, and the extra tissue, blood, and unfertilized egg will all pass out of the body through the vagina. This fluid is known as your period.

The amount of time between periods is what's known as your menstrual cycle. So, the first day you start bleeding marks the first day of your cycle. The average cycle is about 28 days long, while some girls might experience cycles anywhere between 24 and 29 days long. If there's one thing you've picked up so far in this chapter, it's that we're all different. This holds true to periods as well.

While an "irregular period" might sound a little freaky, I promise it's nothing to worry about—generally speaking. To be "irregular" is really anything that is not "regular" to you. If you've just started menstruating, nothing will seem normal at first, and the length and flow will probably vary the first couple of cycles while your new body figures itself out. But after some time, you will get used to your cycle and what to expect. You might even know exactly when it's coming—without a calendar!

Menstrual cramps often signal the start of your period. For some girls, cramps are barely noticeable, while other girls might miss school or other activities each month because the cramps are so painful. If you find yourself in the group of "I can't leave my house for two days each month" crowd, have no fear. There are a lot of steps you can take to lessen the pain, such as changing what you eat, increasing your activity levels, and other tips I'll share in a moment, but let's first discuss other growing pains that may accompany your transition to womanhood.

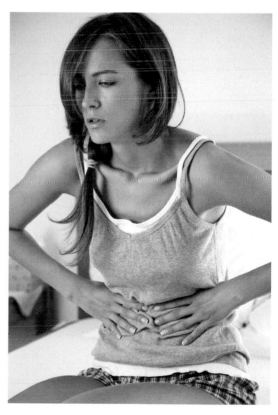

Identity Crisis

Growth spurts are probably nothing new to you. As a kid, you had a major growth spurt between the ages of three and five. While you might not remember exactly what it felt like, you continued to grow at a pace of about two and a half inches per year. When you hit puberty, your body experiences another significant growth spurt. This sudden growth usually takes place between the ages of 10 and 14. And just as you're beginning to fill out upwards, you're going to start filling out outwards as well. With the growth of your breasts, hips, and thighs, your body will start transforming from that of a child, to that of a more curvy woman.

You might know some kids in your class that are close to a foot taller— or a foot shorter than you. Or maybe some girls came back from break with adult-sized boobs, while other girls are still as flat as pancakes. Are your hips stick-straight, while your best friend has some serious curves that have all the boys talking? All of these differences in development rates are normal parts of growing up. Everyone will go through puberty at her own pace, and come out looking just as she was meant to. Make it a point not to compare yourself to your friends and other classmates or teammates. While you're jealous of someone's height, they might be embarrassed of it.

Speaking of being embarrassed, isn't oily hair, acne, and body odor the worst? While most teens experience these problems, it doesn't seem to make them any easier to deal with. You can thank your overly active glands for these issues. Each hair that grows out of your body has its very own sebaceous (or oil) gland. During puberty, these glands go into overdrive producing way more oil than the glands are used to. This excess oil leaves your hair looking dirty and your face dotted with zits...or even your chest and back since all of these surfaces have hair—and ultimately oil glands.

So what exactly is a pimple? Just because an oil gland is producing excess oil doesn't necessarily mean you will have a zit. Acne is an accumulation of oil, dead skin cells, and bacteria in the pore, which causes inflammation. Ever pop a zit? That white stuff that comes out is the bacteria and pus that your body makes to protect itself from infection.

Body odor is the result of overactive sweat glands. You've obviously perspired prior to puberty, but once you're going through the change, those sweat glands not only produce more sweat, they're now pumping out different chemicals which cause a stronger smelling odor. For some girls this smell is barely noticeable, while other girls may feel like everyone in the room is getting a whiff. If you've just started experiencing these funky smells, start your battle of the stench by taking a bath or shower each day. This can help wash away bacteria that could be making the smells worse. Remember to wash under your arms, your feet, and your "downstairs" as well. All of these areas are pumping out new scents. Also be sure to wear clean clothes, socks, and underwear daily. Just because you got three days out of your favorite cartoon socks as a kid, doesn't mean you can get away with that now.

If these methods don't lead to a better smelling you, it might be time to think about a deodorant or antiperspirant. If you don't smell bad in the first place, don't worry about an added layer of protection just yet. For those of you who do, be aware of what kind of products you're buying and putting on your body. Keep in mind, anything you rub into your skin (the largest organ you have) gets absorbed and enters your bloodstream. A lot of products out there contain nasty chemicals that you probably don't want floating around your system on the daily. I'll cover some Primal-friendly products to use in the Teen Puberty Must-Haves section!

How Your Lifestyle Impacts You

Food affects your body in more ways than you realize. Sure it tastes great, fills you up, and gives you energy, but food—and more specifically the right kinds of food—does a ton behind the scenes. Let's take a deeper look at how the foods you eat change the way you feel and how they specifically impact puberty.

In Chapter One, I discussed how certain foods like grains, starches, legumes, soy, sugar, bad fats, and even processed foods cause inflammation, as well as the importance of balancing your omega-6:omega-3 ratio (ideal is 1:1). There are also other factors that induce inflammation in your body such as:

- Poor sleeping habits
- Sedentary lifestyle
- Increased stress
- Poor gut health
- Too little sun exposure (vitamin D)

...and the list goes on. So why should you care about inflammation? Cramps. Pimples. Colds. Need I continue? Inflammation can make your periods so much more painful. It can also make your acne condition worse, since pimples are instigated by inflammation; as well as compromise the function of your immune system, making you more likely to get sore throats, colds, and whatever else is blowing through school each season.

Who loves cramps? Not I. If you find your period is interfering with your day-to-day life (like missing a day of school each month at the start of your period), then it's time to get serious and eliminate, or at least lessen, the problem the best you can. With an anti-inflammatory paleo diet that eliminates irritants such as grains, starches, legumes, soy, sugar, and so on, you will be well on your way to painless periods. Focus on a vitamin-rich diet that includes quality meats, vegetables, fruits, and healthy fats.

Exercise is another important factor of your lifestyle that can affect your level of monthly cramping. Okay, I totally get that when you're curled up in the fetal position with the worst cramps of your life, the last thing you want to do is exercise—but trust me. Exercise releases endorphins into your body, which are natural feel-good hormones. So get yourself off the couch and go for a walk, get some sun, and take control of your body. Don't let it control you.

All right, enough about cramps. Let's talk about your skin. Did you know that there is a link between vitamin D and acne? So, how do you get more vitamin D? Come on, I know you know this one—the sun! Studies assessing seasonal patterns regarding dermatology office visits show that patients experience higher rates of acne in the winter and lower rates in the summer. It's believed that:

- The sun's warmth can heat and destroy organic compounds in bacteria, thereby preventing the infection of your pores.

- Vitamin D may impact the oil glands by producing proteins with antibacterial properties (cathelicidin).

- Vitamin D strengthens the immune system and can help the body fight acne.

While you get the vast majority of your vitamin D from sunshine, you can also get vitamin D through foods like eggs, fatty fish, and fish oils like salmon, mackerel, and cod liver oil.

Teen Puberty Must-Haves

As you've probably gathered by now, being a teenager is both exciting and a little overwhelming at times. Add puberty into the mix and even simple things can feel totally complex. For this reason, I've compiled some must-haves that will make your life so much easier. Stock up on these goodies, and I promise puberty won't be as tricky as the algebra homework you keep putting off!

Pads, Tampons, Menstrual Cups

Whether you chose to use a pad, tampon, or cup, is up to you. If you're new to these products, you might not have a preference yet or even know what some of them are, so let's discuss...

A lot of girls start with pads. Pads are made from an absorbent material and basically stick to your underwear like a giant, absorbent sticker. They come in all shapes and sizes, with or without wings, and some even have added deodorant. The style you choose depends a lot upon your flow. Most girls like using pads when they first get their periods because pads are worn on the outside of the body and it's easy to see when they need changing. When buying pads, be sure to look for brands that use natural products, or opt for reusable cloth pads that aren't full of a bunch of chemicals and mystery items. Most pads need to be changed every three to four hours (check the instructions that come inside the package to know for sure, as some brands may vary).

Some girls prefer to use tampons because they're more discreet in their pocket or purse. Tampons function in a similar manner to pads in the sense that they absorb blood, however, tampons go inside your body. This can be a little intimidating for new users. Some girls are afraid tampons will get lost inside the body, or that they won't be able to pee while wearing a tampon. Some girls just don't like the fact that they can't see when it's time to change their tampon.

Let's dispel some of these myths. For starters, it's absolutely impossible to lose a tampon inside your body. Your vagina may seem like a mysterious place to you at times, but it's physically impossible for an object to go anywhere but out the way it came in. Your cervix is located at the top of your vagina and it's way too tiny for a tampon to fit through, so don't worry about losing anything inside of you. Wearing a tampon does not change the way you urinate. Urine collects in your bladder and exits your body through your urethra. Your urethra and vagina are two very different channels, and a tampon will not interfere with the way you use the restroom. As for not knowing when to change your tampon, they typically need to be changed every four to six hours. Again, when trying a new brand, be sure to read the instructions. If you're having a heavy flow, you might have to change your tampon more often.

> ### ⑪ Smarty Pants:
>
> You should never wear a tampon longer than instructed because doing so can increase the risk of a serious condition called toxic shock syndrome (or TSS). TSS is a bacterial infection whose symptoms include fever, vomiting or diarrhea, muscle aches, weakness or dizziness, and a rash that looks like a sunburn. Tampons with higher absorbency levels may carry a higher risk of getting TSS. While it's a very rare condition, if you experience symptoms like these while wearing a tampon, remove it immediately and tell someone who can take you to the closet emergency room.

Just like pads, tampons can also contain chemicals or other artificial "ingredients" such as:

- Pesticides from conventionally grown cotton, which uses more insecticides than any other crop. (Nearly 25 percent of insecticides used worldwide.)

- Chemicals like artificial color, polyester, and adhesives that have been linked to hormone disruption, cancer, birth defects, dryness, and infertility.

- Latex (take note if you have a latex allergy).

- GMOs (genetically modified organisms; the same stuff you're avoiding in your food), which have been linked to leaky gut syndrome, allergies, and inflammation.

- Crude oil plastic and chlorine-bleached wood pulp.

I mean seriously, whoever thought it was a good idea to put this junk inside a woman's vagina was insane. And the real kicker: pad companies are not required to list ingredients on the box because pads are considered "medical devices" and aren't inserted into your body. Many brands of tampons do list some ingredients on the package, but full disclosure isn't mandatory because the FDA protects proprietary ingredients and formulas. In addition to all the nasty stuff tampons can contain, they also disrupt your pH levels by absorbing discharge and good bacteria...not to mention, they're a breeding ground for bacteria. Yikes!

Aside from health concerns, pads and tampons also create a ton of waste that is bad for the environment, and they cost a lot of money over time too. Consider this: If the average woman menstruates for 40 years and uses approximately 20 feminine products per cycle (240 total each year), she will use 9,600 pads or tampons in her lifetime (although some studies show most women actually use closer to 15,000). At about $0.25 a pop, that's $5 a month, $60 per year, or anywhere between $2,400 and $3,750 for a lifetime of feminine products. And what does the waste of 15,000 pads or tampons look like? Right now there are roughly 100 million women menstruating in the United States, disposing of 12 billion pads into landfills and flushing seven million tampons (plus all the packaging) into the sewer systems each year. We're just talking about the amount of waste created in the US alone. Imagine how bad this problem is on a global scale, or how bad it's going to be a couple decades from now—considering it takes, oh...*only 500 years for these things to decompose!*

Right about now you're probably wondering what the heck you're supposed to do when you get your period. You don't want to put unnatural products inside your body that can potentially make you sick, and you care about the environmental impact. But do you have a choice?

Wait...you want me to put that where?

Well, duh. Of course you have a choice. I wouldn't have told you about all that bad stuff if I didn't have a better solution! The answer is: menstrual cups. I only recently discovered these handy cups, which is a real shame because they're awesome. There are a handful of different brands available on the market: The DivaCup, The Keeper, Lunette, and MoonCup to name a few. As with any product, it's up to you to try different ones and see what works best. Since I have found great success with The DivaCup, that's the brand I'm going to focus on here.

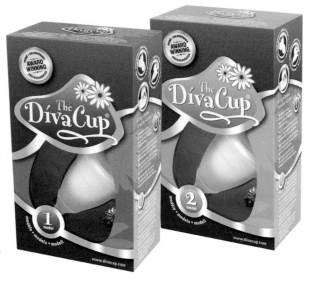

The DivaCup is a reusable, bell-shaped menstrual cup made from healthcare grade silicone. It's worn internally and sits low in the vaginal canal, collecting rather than absorbing your menstrual flow. Since it collects instead of absorbs, it doesn't take away any of your body's natural lubricant or good bacteria. It can be worn for a maximum of 10 to 12 hours before it needs to be washed and rinsed a minimum of two to three times daily. If the idea of washing it at school freaks you out, remember that if you inserted The DivaCup in the morning before leaving for school, you won't need to empty it until dinnertime! And because The DivaCup is totally leak-free when used properly, you don't have to worry about any panicked bathroom trips to survey the leak damage after a sudden "surge" in your flow. Whew!

So, you've got this thing "up there" collecting blood all day; you're probably worried about it smelling bad, right? News flash: menstrual flow only develops an odor when it's exposed to air. Pads are in contact with air throughout the day—that's why those suckers can get stinky. Tampons aren't as bad since they're worn internally (other than the string), but they can still create odor. Since the DivaCup isn't exposed to air at all, you've got nothing to worry about.

What about, umm…mess? Is it, well, icky when you take it out and empty it? Not really. It is, of course, a little more "hands on" than traditional disposable means; however, The DivaCup is surprisingly clean and comfortable once you take the time to learn how to use it. Not to mention, it allows you to learn more about your monthly flow by the convenient ounces and milliliters measurement feature. The DivaCup can hold one full ounce of flow, and the average woman only flows about one to two ounces per cycle.

Not only is a menstrual cup a perfect solution to keeping yucky chemicals out of your body, but it also keeps a ton of waste out of landfills and sewers. And what about those thousands of dollars spent on disposable pads and tampons over a woman's lifetime? The average menstrual cup will run you anywhere between 20 to 40 bucks and are recommended to be replaced annually, but can last longer with proper care. Yup, you read that right—it can last a few years!

For more information on The DivaCup, please visit divacup.com or google search "menstrual cup" to find the brand that's best for you.

Deodorant and Antiperspirant

There are two different products people commonly use under their arms to avoid smelling gross: deodorant and antiperspirant. Deodorant is used to mask odor, while antiperspirants block sweat from being produced by using chemicals, primarily aluminum. The aluminum in antiperspirants works by swelling your pores shut to prevent the release of sweat from your sweat glands. Many health-conscious people agree that it's not a good idea to allow any metals into your bloodstream (and will not use antiperspirant for this reason), even though experts assert that using antiperspirant is not at all dangerous. I'd suggest that you start with a deodorant, and if you experience the annoying problem of moisture under your armpits, you can use a stronger product that contains antiperspirant agents. Just don't apply antiperspirant right after you shave, since it might be more likely to be absorbed into the bloodstream at that time.

Many deodorants have dyes and fragrances that target young girls with colorful package designs, trendy magazine ads, and even TV commercials featuring super stylish teens acting like they're having the time of their lives. (All thanks to their deodorant, of course!) While some girls may be cool with these ingredients, others may have a nasty allergic reaction and experience skin irritation, inflammation, and tenderness. Bottom line: if daily showers aren't cutting it when it comes to odor, look for deodorants made with 100 percent natural scents and that are free of sulfate, phosphate, and paraben. (Look at the labels to be sure.) Hit up a good health food store or search online, since major brands on the shelves of grocery stores and pharmacies are typically full of chemicals.

Facial Cleanser

Thanks to those overactive oil glands, you'll need a really good facial cleanser to wash away excess oil, dirt, and makeup and prevent infection—aka acne. With washes and scrubs for oily, dry, and normal skin, spot treatments, toners, masks, and cleansing cloths, the endless options can feel like overkill. The key is to keep it simple. Remember that just like deodorants, facial cleansers can contain chemicals that may cause more harm than good. Safe and natural facial cleansers can be found in health food stores, online, and you know I've got a facial cleanser or two up my sleeve in Chapter Seven.

Healing Heat

Cramps are no joke. If light exercise or relaxing isn't helping, try the magic of heat! A heating pad or a warm soak in the tub can help your muscles relax and lessen the intensity of your cramps. If you choose a bath over a heating pad, consider adding some essential oils to the tub to help that relaxation go a little further. Come on, you deserve it!

Calendar/Period App

You do not want to be unprepared when your period comes. Keeping a stash of pads or tampons in your purse and locker is a fine idea, but that won't save you if Mother Nature decides to surprise you in the middle of history class. To make sure this never happens to you, keep track of your cycle! It's easy to do and it will keep you in the loop. You can mark the days on a calendar or your school planner (you can use a code word or just highlight the days of your period if you don't want anyone to know what you're tracking) or better yet, download an app. There are a ton of period apps that you can download for free and they will track when you got your last period, when the next one is coming, and even the days that you're most fertile.

Your period doesn't have to suck.

Relationships: Family, Friends, and Boys

Okay, you've really had it now! Your family is being totally nosy, your friends are acting dramatic, and boys—wow, you just can't understand what's going through their heads, if anything at all! Sound familiar? Let's take a step back, a deep breath, and dive deeper into these relationships.

Let's start with family. Is your mom asking you way too many questions about your period? Did your older sister really just ask you about stealing her tampons right in front of your friends? Did your crazy aunt ask if you've outgrown your training bra yet? As annoying or embarrassing as the questions may be, did you ever take a minute to think why they're asking you? I guarantee they're not trying to make you upset. Every female member of your family went through these same changes, and they remember just how difficult it can be at times. They are there for you, and quite often what might feel like an interrogation is just a way of reaching out and making sure that you feel comfortable coming to them if you have any questions. I bet if you open up those lines of communication and show them that you're happy to come to them for guidance when you need it, it won't feel like they're butting into your personal space as much.

Now let's take a look at your friends. Are certain friends acting possessive of other friends? Are you getting a hard time from one girl for being too boy crazy, while another girl thinks you aren't boy crazy enough? How about that friend who keeps fighting with you online and ratting you out to your bestie? I mean what the heck is going on? Is everyone insane?! Or have you become just as dramatic, irrational, over-the-top, crazy, and unreasonable as they have? If you feel this way about them, they just might feel the same way about you.

Let's reassess. You've got a ton of different hormones coursing through your veins, new body parts popping up over night, and sometimes you smell like a locker room. That's a lot to handle, but remember they're experiencing all of these things too. Cut them some slack, and cut yourself some slack as well. Talk to your girlfriends about the changes you're experiencing and you'll probably realize you're not in this alone. Also remember that puberty is not a competition. Be kind to others. We all have our own struggles and insecurities. There's no point in adding more stress to puberty than it already brings on its own.

You should already feel a little better with some new perspective about your friends and family. And while I have you in this compassionate and rational space, I think it's safe to move on to our last topic—boys. Remember, I said be nice!

Boys can be a curious species. They can be great at saying the wrong things, and they can do an excellent job of picking on you. Other times, you can just sit back and watch as they make fools of themselves. But please don't forget, they're going through puberty too, and puberty for a guy can be a very different ride.

For starters, they go through puberty later than girls—not until they're between 9 and 14 years old. As tempting as it may be, this is no reason to make fun of them. Boys can't help when they go through puberty, just like girls can't help when they do. Since boys start later than girls, this means that girls might grow taller than boys for a while. Girls might start looking more like women before boys start looking like men. Girls will also start to mature emotionally earlier than boys. This is all completely normal, and hopefully understanding this helps you have a little more patience for boys and their antics.

There are also other changes that boys experience that can be embarrassing for them. For example, before their voices change (or permanently become deeper), they may experience a weird in-between stage where they seem to have no control over the voice and it cracks a lot and sounds really raspy. Girls also go through this, but it's not nearly as dramatic or noticeable.

Boys also start growing hair like you—but more of it. In addition to pubic hair, hair sprouts up on their legs, chest, armpits, and face. They too start experiencing acne and body odor. But the most embarrassing thing boys have to deal with that you obviously don't, is an entirely different experience with their "downstairs." During puberty, with all the new hormones swimming around in their bodies, boys start getting a lot more erections. An erection occurs when blood rushes into the penis, making it hard. For adult men, this usually happens before they have sex, but for boys, erections can happen anywhere. Sometimes they might be excited sexually, such as when thinking about a certain girl. Other times, their hormones are running so wild, that erections can happen when they least expect it, and have nothing to do with being sexually excited. We're talking randomly at the end of English class, during football drills, while walking the dog after school, or when they first wake up.

For a guy, a surprise erection can be a humiliating experience. Sometimes you just can't help but notice what is usually called a "bulge" in someone's pants. It's really important that girls understand that guys can't help it when it happens, and it's only a part of growing up. Just like you wouldn't like

it if a boy made fun of you if you started your period in the middle of class and had a bloodstain on your jeans, a boy would be mortified if you made fun of him for getting an erection.

Beyond the physical changes that you can see, inside the brain guys and girls experience a new and funny feeling too: crushes. When you were younger, you might not have had a second thought about a boy passing you on the playground. Now when you see a certain boy you might feel really warm, nervous, jittery, and generally unsure of yourself. You might even notice that your palms or armpits start to sweat. Or maybe your best friend has started talking 24/7 about a guy she thinks is cute. Boys experience this too, of course, but because of the physical timeline differences I mentioned earlier, they might not go girl crazy until a grade or two later than most girls.

Whew! That was a lot of intense information, but hopefully it all helps you feel pretty normal and comfortable with the new experiences that are ahead or that you're currently facing. Just remember that you will always have family, friends, teachers, and other adults around you that love and care about you. There is no challenge you have to face alone, if you don't want to.

The feeling when a crush likes you back...

What Is Puberty?

Girls begin puberty, or the process by which adolescents reach sexual maturity and become capable of reproduction, between the ages of 7 and 14 and end between the ages of 15 and 17.

Hormones Galore

Your brain releases gonadotropin-releasing hormone, or GnRH. It travels to your pituitary gland and there, luteinizing hormone (LH) and follicle-stimulating hormone (FSH) are released. LH and FSH work in your ovaries to produce estrogen. These three hormones work together to help your body mature and prepare you for pregnancy.

Upstairs/Downstairs

The Tanner Scale is a five-stage process that tracks breast and pubic hair development.

That Time of the Month

Your first period is called "menarche" and doesn't occur until your reproductive system has fully matured. When an egg is released, it travels down a fallopian tube towards the uterus, a process called ovulation. A couple of days before ovulation, your uterine walls line with extra blood and tissue. If the egg becomes fertilized, it will attach to the walls of the uterus and you will become pregnant. If the egg doesn't become fertilized, it and the extra tissue and blood will exit your body through the vagina. This is your period. The amount of time between periods is your menstrual cycle, and the average cycle lasts about 28 days.

Identity Crisis

During puberty, you go through a lot of external changes too. Growth spurts, new curves, oily hair, acne, and body odor are each a part of development.

How Our Lifestyle Impacts Us

Inflammation through the foods you eat can increase the level of pain you experience from cramps. Eliminating foods like grains, starches, legumes, soy, sugar, bad fats, and processed foods will help lessen or even eliminate period cramps. Working out can help too, by releasing endorphins, or "feel good" hormones to minimize pain. Additionally, vitamin D can help with acne.

Teen Puberty Must-Haves

Every teen girl needs the right kind of pad, tampon, or menstrual cup for her cycle, but it takes experimentation to know what works the best for you. Deodorants, antiperspirants, and facial cleansers can be tricky, and it's best to avoid products that contain dyes, fragrances, sulfates, phosphates, and/or parabens. Heating pads or a hot bath can relax your muscles and reduce cramping. And always keep a calendar or download a period app so you can track your monthly cycle and never be caught off guard.

Relationships: Family, Friends, and Boys

Your family has been though the changes you're going through and can be there for you when you need them the most. Don't take their questions to heart—they're not being nosy! Your friends are going through the exact same changes that you are and can be great allies if you work together and don't gang up on each other. Boys are also going through changes, but very different ones. Be mindful of others and don't let your hormones get the best of you!

Chapter Five

Motivation 101: It's a Date!

If Your Family Freaks

So now you're totally amped. You've got your diet dialed, your fitness set, and everything else roaring to go! It all feels so perfect and you're ready to be a modern-day cave girl. One catch—your parents aren't feeling it. Not only are they not feeling it—they're pretty much telling you, "NO WAY!" Hmm, what now? Why don't your parents understand? Let's take a look at a few things that could be standing in your way.

For starters, what do your parents eat? Are they junk food junkies just like you were before picking up this book? There's a good chance they just don't understand what it means to be paleo. Look at this as an opportunity to get some quality family time in, and maybe win over a few allies too. Share what you've learned with them. Back up your facts with some cold hard scientific evidence. Let them read this book, or send them over to Mark's Daily Apple and let them see what this lifestyle is all about. There's a pretty good chance they're in the dark about this kind of stuff just as much as you used to be. Assuming they also grew up

under the false impression that "fat is bad," it's understandable that they could be hesitant to embrace a totally different eating style. New things can be scary, even for adults. Help them understand what paleo is all about, and there's a chance they'll go beyond supporting your decision to actually joining you!

So you've given every bit of information you could find on Primal living to your parents. You've made charts and graphs. You've built a time machine and showed them how great this lifestyle is going to be for your entire family—and they still don't support you. In fact, they disagree with it all. Now what? Since they're your parents and they put a roof over your head and food on the table, you might feel like you have no choice but to live in "grain pain" the rest of your life. But have no fear; there are some easy Primal choices you can make to live closer to the lifestyle you want, while maintaining peace in your home.

- Ask for vegetables at every meal—bonus if they're green.

- Skip sugary drinks like soda, juice, or flavored milk—even if everyone else is drinking them.

- Strive for a protein source like eggs for breakfast instead of oatmeal or cereal.

- Skip or take much smaller portions of rice, bread, corn, beans, etc. at meal times and instead add more vegetables to your plate.

- Eat until you're satisfied, which is different than "full." (You shouldn't have to unbutton your jeans after a meal!)

- Avoid candy, sugary snacks, and heavily processed foods that come in wrappers and boxes.

- Pack your lunch often and fill your bag/box with as much fresh food as possible.

These tips aren't just Primal-friendly; they're pretty much common sense to any-one eating healthy. Your parents might be concerned about the amount of fat you want to consume or the whole-grains that will be missing from your diet, but they can't argue with you about wanting to eat more vegetables and less sugar. Pick your battles and take small steps. I bet once they see your acne disappear, your sleeping habits improve, and your overall mood change, they might see there's more to this whole "caveman thing" after all.

Let's say it plays out like this: your parents total-ly understand the diet and fully support you, but the only problem is money. They're afraid that buying high quality meat and produce for the whole family will be pricey. Or maybe they plan to continue eating a Standard American Diet (SAD) while supporting your paleo ways and that means buying way more groceries than usual. I totally get it! Changing your grocery shopping routine can feel stressful, but a lot of people do Primal on a budget. Let's check out some cheap tricks that might be helpful for your family:

- Review the produce discussed in Chapter One in the "Non-Organic Approved Produce" and "Organic Approved Produce" lists. Memorize them. Never pay premium prices for foods that you don't need to. If you can't afford organic, don't buy organic. But also remember that at the end of the day, eating non-or-ganic strawberries is always better than eating donuts.

- If you don't want to pay top dollar for organic meat, fowl, or fish, get leaner cuts. The toxins and the bad junk in an animal's body are stored in fat. If you buy conventionally raised animals, opt for the skin-off, fat-trimmed versions to less-en your exposure to the offensive stuff.

- Give back to your community and hit up farmers markets and local butchers. Sometimes you can find better prices, and when the prices are the same as those of the big chain stores, the quality of food you can buy locally is almost always better. Not to mention, you can often negotiate prices with an individual—bargaining never happens in line at the grocery!

- Buy in bulk, cook in bulk. This will not only save you money but also your precious time. (Your time is worth something too, you know.)

- Plant a garden. To quote Ron Finley, a popular urban gardener in South Central Los Angeles, "Growing your own food is like printing your own money." Sit and think about the power behind that statement. If you don't have the money to buy what you want to eat, grow what you want to eat—all at a fraction of the cost and with peace of mind knowing it's organic and grown with love.

- Don't have room for a garden? Plant a small indoor herb garden (every little bit helps) or join a CSA (Community Supported Agriculture). A CSA is a community of farmers that pair up with local people just like you. When you join, you receive a box of fresh, farm grown veggies each week. It's like having a Netflix membership but you get awesome local produce instead of videos that encourage you to become a couch potato.

- Eat less. Okay, sorry if that one caught you off guard. But if you're stuffing your face 24/7, day and night, it might be time to lay off the snacking for a bit, right? (Even if it is with Primal-friendly treats!) You don't need to eat an abundance of food every day, especially when you have built up some momentum eating paleo and are better at burning body fat. Besides, all of that food costs money. So if you're trying to save some cash, eat until you're satisfied—don't just devour everything in sight!

Look at all the "money" she grew!

Now it's time to discuss the harder topics. What if your parents don't want you eating Primal because it's against their religion or goes against their cultural background? There are a number of religions around the world that have dietary restrictions.

- Buddhists are typically vegetarian, and some avoid the "five pungent spices"—onions, garlic, scallions, chives, and leeks.

- Catholics generally do not eat meat (and sometimes fast) on Ash Wednesday, Good Friday, and all Fridays during Lent.

- Hindus often are vegetarian, and if not, they at least avoid beef.

- Jews most often stay away from pork and pork products, shellfish, meat and dairy at the same meal, and birds of prey.

- Mormons typically stay away from coffee, tea, or other caffeinated beverages, and also avoid excessive amounts of meat.

- Muslims normally do not consume pork or pork products, birds of prey, or carnivorous animals. Additionally, overeating is strongly discouraged and naturally grown food is ideal.

And that's just the tip of the iceberg. There are many more religions around the world that practice dietary restrictions in the name of faith. So what happens if you and your family are vegetarian for religious purposes and you suddenly want to eat meat to achieve optimum health? It seems you've stumbled upon quite the predicament, huh? Well, let's start with this: being paleo doesn't mean you have to eat every piece of meat within a five-block radius of you. Let's stop worrying so much about what you can't eat, and instead focus on what you can.

- What kind of vegetarian are you? If ovo, lacto, or pesco are a prefix to your version of vegetarianism, that means you are allowed eggs (ovo), dairy (lacto), or fish (pescetarian). Learn to love these items, as they will be your ideal sources of protein.

- Protein shakes can help with protein intake. My favorite is Vanilla Coconut Crème Primal Fuel. With a neutral flavor like vanilla, you can add anything—fruit, nuts, dark chocolate, coffee, etc.—and make any flavor you're craving.

- In addition to loading up on leafy greens, you'll need to consume more starch like yams, sweet potatoes, potatoes, other root tubers, and fruit, simply for the calories.

- Be nuts about nuts for a good source of fat and protein.

- Lentils are the least offensive legumes for added protein, and quinoa is a high protein pseudo-grain in disguise.

Moral of the story: focus on paleo food that is vegetarian friendly like coconut, fruits, vegetables, tubers, nuts, and when faced with grains and legumes, choose the less scary kinds like lentils and quinoa. This will keep you and your family's religious beliefs in check, and allow you to follow a healthier lifestyle. If your wishes are to throw your dietary restrictions out the door, then that's a bigger conversation to have with your parents. If your parents and faith aren't too strict, you might be able to compromise on some things and meet in the middle. Otherwise you might just have to do your best and wait until you're old enough and out of your parents' home to buy and cook the types of food you feel are right for you.

Maneuvering around cultural backgrounds and foods native to your ethnicity can be a little tricky as well. Rice is a staple for many Asian cultures. Rice, beans, and tortillas are the foundation of so many Mexican dishes. When you think of Italy, you probably picture all kinds of breads and pastas. Know what I mean? If your mom is cranking out stacks of freshly pressed tortillas for dinner, how are you supposed to say no? Odds are you don't even want to. Sinking your teeth into that warm corn shell not only tastes great, but it's also what you grew up on. It's comfort food. It's a bonding moment and a tradition in your family. How could this be a bad thing? Truth is, if there are foods in your life that you just can't (or won't) let go of, that's okay. Just show some restraint when it comes to mealtime. If you usually scarf down five tortillas, try eating just two, and add a little extra meat and veggies to your plate. You'll still have all the delicious spices and flavors of mom's cooking, but with less of the bad stuff.

You might also want to consider getting creative with updated recipes. I recently made the absolute best empanadas for my family—and they were 100 percent

Primal approved. Instead of using wheat flour (which contains the highly offensive anti-nutrient gluten), I substituted with tapioca and potato flours. They were crispy on the outside, chewy on the inside, and filled with all of my favorite meats and cheeses. I also make a killer Primal pizza with almond flour and arrowroot instead of traditional ingredients. Honestly, the texture and taste are even better than most of the pizza crusts made with flour (gluten). (Sorry if I'm making you drool, but have no fear—the Cave Crave Pizza recipe is in Chapter Seven!) If you talk to your parents about how important this is to you, I bet they'd be open to making small changes like this. And hey, you'll never know unless you ask!

How to Deal

Having a healthy home front and allies under your own roof is super important. When mom and dad help you with meals and take you to your games, and your sibling motivates you in ways you could never have imagined, it's easy to feel on top of the world. But let's be real—home life is really only half of your life. The rest of the time you're exposed to other people at school, on your sports teams, at the mall, in the media, online, and the list goes on. And while it's nice to think that all the people you come in contact with throughout your day have your best intentions in mind, quite often they don't. Okay, most of the people in your social circle might, but odds are you've had a negative interaction (or many) with someone directly or even indirectly. We all have.

Can't we all just get along already?

Bullies

Bullying is seriously uncool behavior. Experts agree that bullying can have a lifelong negative affect on someone's personality and self-confidence. Bullying comes in many forms: it can be making fun of the way someone dresses or looks, or teasing an entire group of friends. Others take heat because of their religion, ethnicity, height, weight, sexual orientation, and so on. Sometimes bullies go beyond verbal attacks and resort to violence. This could be anything from tripping someone in the hallway, shoving someone in the locker room, punching someone, or even committing a sexual assault. The drama doesn't end there. Cyberbullying (bullying through online communication) has become a real issue. Sending vicious texts, emails, or posting awful gossip on Facebook, Twitter, or other social media platforms all counts as cyberbullying.

Have you ever been a victim of cyberbullying? If so, how did it make you feel? Nervous and anxious? Sick to your stomach? Unable to rise and shine because you dread the day? These emotional and physical reactions can make a teen feel socially isolated, with low self esteem and battling depression—she may even be considering suicide.

If you or a friend is the victim of bullying, don't keep it to yourself. Tell an adult, like a parent, coach, teacher, counselor, or neighbor—anyone in a position of authority who can listen and take some action to stop it. Too often, bullying escalates to scary levels, especially when the tormenter thinks you're just going to take his or her crap and not tell anyone. It's absolutely vital to report problems before they turn physical or cause serious emotional harm.

What if the problem hasn't quite escalated to the point where you need to tell an adult? What if someone makes you uncomfortable, but you're not even sure if it counts as bullying? What if you told an adult about some bullying and the problem continues? Here are a few tips for dealing with bullies and bullying:

• Grab the bull by the horns: talk directly to the bully in a safe environment where others are present and nothing bad can happen. Keep calm and lead by example, showing them that you're in control of your emotions. If a face-to-face convo has you nervous, slip them a note in class, message them on Facebook, or just start with a simple "hi!" when you pass them in the hallway. Sometimes all bullies want is attention and recognition, and don't know a healthy way to connect with others.

- Confidence is key: bullies often target "easy prey" and pick on peers who are shy, awkward, or easily uncomfortable or embarrassed. So stand tall, and don't give that bully any material to work with.

- Don't give them what they want: the typical goal of a bully is to get a response out of you—seeing you get angry, fearful, or annoyed. If you don't respond to the childish behavior, the bully might just move along.

- Laugh it off: sometimes this can catch the bully off guard, since their main priority is to have control over your emotions. If you give them the opposite reaction, they may not know how to respond. When someone makes a joke at my expense, I've found it effective to laugh right along with them. It's never what they expect, so it redirects them from trying to be mean to maybe actually making an authentic connection with you. Or moving on!

- Safety in numbers: if you see someone getting bullied, speak up. Often times your peers want to speak up too, but they're afraid of becoming a target if they do. If a number of people come together, one bully can quickly become outnumbered. A small shift caused by a few voices speaking up might soon make bullying uncool at your school or in your neighborhood.

- Mirror, mirror on the wall: never fight back with more of the same. If you throw insults, resort to name-calling, or attack a bully physically, you're no better than the bully. Remember, if someone is getting harmed physically, the only reasonable thing to do is to get an authority figure involved.

After constant harassment, some teens don't know what to do, other than to take on the roll of the bullies themselves. Sometimes it feels like this is the only answer—but that's just like fighting fire with fire. So what the heck are you supposed to do if you realize *you're* the bully? Once you've been a certain way for so long it can feel like a rough transition into something else, but don't lose hope. It's easier than you might think.

What if you realize you're the bully?

Instead of going to school with a negative outlook, try to see the positive. If that's hard for you to do, fake it until you make it. Tell someone they look nice, laugh at someone's joke, or pick up the paper someone just dropped in the hallway. You can change the way people see you just by being a better version of you. I bet the people at school will like this new you and include you on their team in gym, have you sit with them at lunch, or even call you after school. Teens just like to have a good time and be happy, so join the fun and don't be such a grump!

Maybe your reasons for bullying go deeper than this—perhaps you're not just unhappy, but your home life is rough. Maybe the reason you put people down is because that's the norm at home. If this is the case, talk to someone. If you can't reach out to your parents, there are plenty of adults who would be glad to help you. Speak with a teacher, counselor, coach, or family friend.

Dealing with Peer Pressure

Peer pressure can make you do crazy things that you would never normally consider doing or saying. The fear of sticking out or looking like a wimp is never a fun idea, especially when it's in front of one of the popular girls at school or your latest crush. Peer pressure happens to everyone and can lead to foolish activities, like stealing, doing drugs, drinking alcohol, being reckless behind the wheel, engaging in inappropriate sexual behavior, lying or cheating in school, and so on.

Think back to the last time you felt pressured by the people around you to do something you didn't think was right or didn't feel ready for. Sometimes peer pressure doesn't just result in actions but shows up in your feelings. You might actually enjoy the lessons in fifth period science class, but some of the kids in class think science is lame so you act like you hate the class too. This might seem harmless at first, but could escalate to you acting out in class, missing homework, doing poorly on tests, or disappointing your favorite teacher, all in the interest of fitting in.

It's good to be aware that peer pressure comes in all shapes and sizes. Here are some tips to help you face peer pressure:

• Hang out with people who think and feel the same way you do about different topics. If you surround yourself with like-minded friends, you'll be less exposed to the pressures others might put on you.

• Listen to your gut. Your initial instinct will almost always lead you to make sensible decisions. If a situation or person makes you feel uncomfortable but you can't decide exactly why, it's probably best to get out of that situation.

- Plan ahead. If you want to go to a football game, the mall, or a party, and you think you'll run into someone who's going to pressure you into doing something you don't want to do, take steps to avoid trouble. Make arrangements to go with a few friends so you won't be singled out, or make an excuse to bail if you experience one-on-one pressure to do something you don't want to.

- Come up with a secret code word or phrase and only let your parents or closest friends in on it. Let them know that if the "secret word" pops up in a conversation or on the phone, that you're in a sticky situation and need their help. By using a code word, the people pressuring you will never even know that you've asked someone else for help right in front of them.

- If peer pressure is forcing you into a dangerous situation, do not hesitate to find an adult and ask for help.

Now that we've covered how to deal with the negative aspects of peer pressure, it's also important to discuss how peer pressure can be a good thing. Maybe you almost didn't try out for the school talent show, but your bestie knew this would be the perfect opportunity for you to show off your killer voice. In this situation, her persistent, "Oh come on, this is your chance to show everyone what you've got!" is a very healthy form of peer pressure that pushes you to better yourself. Even if you're scared or nervous to perform in front of the entire school, you can see how this type of coaxing is different from pressuring you into drinking beer at a party.

Self-Esteem

When you look in the mirror, what do you see? How do you feel? Are you thrilled with your new haircut? Do you love the way your jeans fit? Are your braces annoying, but you love the new straight smile that's forming beneath them? Do you like who you see looking back at you? I hope that your answers are, "YES!" Unfortunately, life isn't always that easy. For some teens, looking in the mirror can feel less than rewarding. Do you wish you were taller or skinnier? Do you long for straight hair instead of what feels like a bird's nest on top of your head? Do you just avoid the mirror in general sometimes?

Self-esteem is all about how you feel about yourself. What are you worth? What do you think you're worth to others? When you have a healthy body image, you tend to have better self-esteem. You feel confidant in who you are, flaws and all. Self-esteem and body image tend to go hand in hand, probably because our culture makes such a big deal about physical beauty and sexuality. It's kind of a bummer that some (or a lot) of our happiness is riding on our looks. I mean, what would life be like if you didn't constantly have to worry about what you look like on the outside and instead all that mattered was what's on the inside?

When you were a kid, body image and self-esteem weren't even on your radar. You were just stoked to run around and play outside with your friends. The goofier someone was, the more fun they seemed, and you didn't have a care in the world. Why all of a sudden does everything change?

For starters, puberty can cause people to struggle for the first time with self-esteem and body issues. As mentioned in Chapter Four, when going through crazy physical changes, it can be tempting to compare yourself with others. Since you know we all develop at our own rate into a very unique finished product, it should be easy to understand that there's no reason to feel like you're competing against one another. Sometimes understanding it's all in your head doesn't make it any easier, though. The deep urge to want to feel accepted and liked among friends—and boys—can easily panic even the most beautiful girl in school.

Why is it that we hold ourselves up against such high standards? Well, a lot of it could have to do with media and celebrities. Look at all the flawless faces gracing the covers of the most popular fashion magazines. They have perfect skin, impeccable hair, the best clothes, and come up with the most clever jokes! The girls at school idolize the top celebs, and the boys drool over them. Hard to not want to be the cover girl, right? Think again. The girl on the cover may seem perfect, but it's really an illusion. Trust me, she is full of flaws just like you and I. Through the magic of Hollywood and airbrushing, here's what you don't see:

- That perfect skin? Hollywood It Girls spend an hour in the makeup chair before the camera even clicks. The images are then processed by a photo editor who magically erases every blemish.

- Her impeccable hair? It takes a professional hairstylist over an hour to sculpt that masterpiece and the photo editor still has to get rid of all the flyaways, and alter the color in post-production.

- Those amazing (and expensive) clothes? They're not hers. They're on loan from the designer for publicity.

- What about her witty, intelligent interview comments? Of course she really said all that, right? Not always. Often a talent's agent or manager works with a publication to make sure what's printed is "in line" with her brand image.

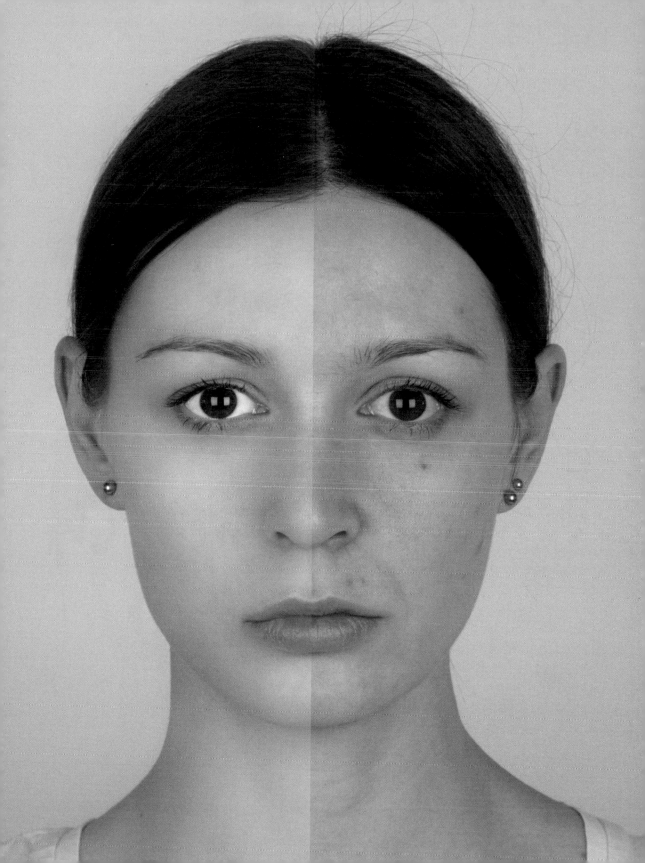

So how on earth do you expect to compete with something that's not even real? That's like being jealous of a unicorn! Never compare yourself to others. After all, the real people in this world are not perfect, and the perfect people aren't even real.

Beyond puberty and celebs, your family can influence your self-esteem as well. Sometimes adults who struggle with their own esteem and body image issues unintentionally take it out on their kids. Have you ever heard, "Your pants are too tight!" or "Why is your hair always in your face?" When parents nitpick the way you look, it can hurt your feelings or make you feel bad about yourself. Sometimes parents just aren't in on the latest fashion trends, you know? And your mom may have just spent the last 10 minutes in front of the mirror berating herself for not being able to fit back in to her "skinny jeans." In other words, what others (even your family) say about your looks has nothing to do with you, and everything to do with them.

In addition to your parents, teens your age can have a negative effect on your self-esteem, even if it's unintended. We have the obvious stuff like bullying and peer pressure, but sometimes even seemingly innocent comments can throw you for a loop. Let's say you want to borrow a shirt from a friend and she says, "Sorry, I don't have any extra large tops!"

Sometimes friends can engage in pettiness that's a little less than innocent, too. Like if you mention how you're struggling in a certain class, and someone at the lunch table says, "I had that class last year, it was sooo easy!" I mean, how's a girl supposed to get ahead with all this negativity? Let's discuss some tips for building healthy self-esteem, holding a positive body image, and generally appreciating your years as a teenager instead of just wishing you were an adult already.

Now that is one magestic unicorn...

- Be positive and optimistic: even if you don't know how, just fake it until you make it. If you repeat positive affirmations about yourself every day, one day you'll believe them. This isn't just jabber; psychologists assert that positive self-talk can have a lasting impact. I'm not talking about harboring fairy tale delusions here, but rather framing your circumstances in the most positive and optimistic light possible. For example, "I'm struggling on this soccer team and upperclassmen are mean to me, but if I keep working hard I know I'll improve and also earn my teammates' respect."

- Love what you've got: and don't stress what you don't. Focusing on the negatives will only make you feel worse. Realize you are the only you in this world. That's pretty darn special, if you ask me.

- Make things happen: if you really want to change something about yourself, put time into the things you can change. Like improving your health, the way you treat others, how smart you are, or the types of people you hang out with. Other variables like how tall you are, who your parents are, and the kind of house you live in are beyond your control. Don't waste your energy worrying about issues like that.

- Change your inner dialogue: you know that voice in your head that says, "You can't do this!" or "You're not good enough!"? We all have it. If your internal dialogue is saying something you don't like, then change it. It might be tough at first, but it's possible. You are the one in control of this ride!

- Reach out: if you're having a tough time feeling positive on your own, try talking to a friend. Or if your situation is too hard to talk about with someone your age, seek out the help of an adult. Sometimes a counselor or therapist can help you make the change you want. If you feel like there's no one to talk to, call a teen crisis hotline or search online for a support network near you.

Dealing with Eating Disorders

There's a good chance you know someone with an eating disorder (sometimes called ED for short). Ninety-five percent of people struggling with an ED are between the ages of 12 and 25 years old. The two most common types of eating disorders are anorexia nervosa and bulimia nervosa. (People usually drop the "nervosa" from the end when talking about eating disorders.) In addition to these common illnesses (yes, an eating disorder is an illness), there are other types of problems both girls and guys can have with food, including binge eating, food phobias, and other issues that relate back to body image disorders. To better understand anorexia and bulimia, let's look at the symptoms and signs of each.

Anorexia (an-oh-rek-see-uh)
This eating disorder revolves around an obsession with controlling body weight and food intake. People struggling with anorexia are often far below the ideal weight for their age and height. To stay so slim, these individuals generally eat much less than they should, and/or exercise excessively. When you boil this ED down to its basic form, often times the obsession is more about coping with emotional problems and lack of self-worth. An anorexic, despite being extremely thin, has a distorted view of herself such that she actually believes she is still carrying excess body fat. Anorexics might weigh themselves often, count or portion foods obsessively, become socially withdrawn, show signs of depression, lack energy, and often feel cold.

Bulimia (buh-lee-me-uh)
This eating disorder is a lot like anorexia, except a bulimic will binge eat and then compensate in dangerous ways like forced vomiting, use of laxatives, excessive exercise, or any combination of these in an effort to neutralize the calories consumed and prevent weight gain. A bulimic will often binge on large quantities of junk food in private, eat until she is incredibly stuffed, and then stick her fingers down her throat until she triggers a gag reflex and vomits the food up. All this can happen in a matter of a couple minutes, unbeknownst to the friends waiting downstairs. People struggling with this ED are generally of average weight or overweight. They might make excuses to go to the restroom immediately following meals, buy laxatives, diuretics, or enemas regularly, exercise obsessively, or become socially withdrawn, especially when a social setting involves food.

Eating disorders are a very serious problem, but don't let all the descriptions freak you out. Maybe you pig out sometimes at a birthday party and then work out the next day to make up for it, or maybe you pay attention to the amount of food you're eating and portion things out a lot. This doesn't mean you have an eating disorder. As long as you maintain an overall healthy relationship with food and yourself, you're probably safe from eating disorders. If you're worried you might have an eating disorder but you aren't sure, the first thing you should do is seek help from a professional.

Now that you understand what eating disorders are, you're probably wondering why some girls develop them? If you want to get super technical, no one knows for sure. There's plenty of research being done to try and answer this question, but until then, there are only theories linked to circumstances in a teen's life, like:

- Increased physical and emotional changes associated with puberty.

- Heightened academic pressure.

- Encouragement to "make weight" or be a certain body type for athletes or dancers—particularly gymnasts, ice skaters, ballet dancers, and long distance runners.

- More peer pressure to fit in or uphold high school standards of beauty.

- A sense of not feeling in control of one's independence.

- Influence of physically extreme celebrities and superficial Hollywood ideals.

- Onset of depression, anxiety, or obsessive-compulsive disorder (OCD).

- There is some evidence that eating disorders may run in families or are a learned behavior.

Do you notice a trend from that list? It looks like a whole lot of teen pressure to me. Pressure to fit in, to be liked, to be ideal, to be perfect. But who the heck gets to decide what perfect is? Let's time travel back 10,000 years ago and see if Grokette struggled with these types of physical pressures.

Back in the pre-civilization days, hunter-gatherer teens still went through puberty and experienced a bunch of physical and emotional changes. They also probably felt a little pressure to help out more around camp with cooking, cleaning, child-care, hunting, and gathering. Beyond that, there are few similarities to the cultural circumstances faced by teens today. Back in the day, teen girls weren't obsessing over being the hottest girl in the village. They weren't learning destructive behavior from their friends and family, and they certainly didn't hate themselves when they looked in the mirror—because they didn't have mirrors! These young, powerful, confident, and strong girls didn't measure their self-worth based on physical appearance. They worked in groups and teams to help their families and communities thrive. Not to mention, everything was a serious matter of life and death back then. We all have an internal instinct to thrive, and disordered eating of any kind would have been a really ridiculous thing to even consider.

Okay, so our hunter-gather ancestors didn't struggle with eating disorders, good for them, but this is the 21st century and eating disorders are a real issue. If you or a friend feels compelled to fit into some idealistic stereotype, let's look at what happens to your body when you develop anorexia or bulimia.

Anorexia Effects	Bulimia Effects
• Fatigue	• Abnormal bowl function
• Dizziness or fainting	• Bloating
• Seizures	• Dehydration
• Brittle nails	• Fainting/Seizures
• Thinning hair or loss of hair	• Fatigue
• Loss of period (amenorrhea)	• Dry skin
• Constipation	• Irregular heartbeat
• Dry skin	• Loss of period (amenorrhea)
• Intolerance of cold	• Tingling of hands or feet
• Lanugo (fine hair on face/body)	• Swollen cheeks/salivary glands
• Irregular heart beat	• Tooth decay/mouth sores
• Low blood pressure	• Muscle cramps
• Dehydration	• Internal bleeding
• Osteoporosis (the loss of bone calcium)	• Infertility
• Paralysis	• Suicide/Self-injury
• Death	• Heart attack
	• Death

Mirrors didn't exist 10,000 years ago...

So tell me, do things like dry skin, constipation, hair loss, and brittle nails sound like the trick to looking like your favorite celebrity or your ideal of perfection? If not, then why take such extreme and misguided measures to try and achieve them? That's not the way to be happy, look healthy, or become successful. If you feel like starving yourself, or think binging and purging is the only answer, please speak to an adult or counselor, or call a teen hotline. It's imperative to talk to anyone who will listen.

Your Wolf Pack

Thanks to the glow of social media from every device in your home, "friends" have a whole new meaning these days. Ten thousand years ago, Grokette's friends were the members of her clan. She had an inner circle, which consisted of about a dozen people that were her closest friends and family. Outside of that was what anthropologists call a social circle. These were people within her hunter-gatherer clan that she interacted with daily and trusted. The social circle

formed a means of protection—a system to learn where to get food, water, shelter; the best techniques for hunting and gathering; raising children; and avoiding danger. However, these relationships within her larger clan were not quite as intimate as those in her inner circle. Grokette's social circle consisted of probably another 25 or so people. The sizes of these circles are what today's behavior psychologists believe is ideal for the human brain to handle successfully. In fact, leading anthropologist Robin Dunbar went through the trouble to actually characterize people in your social circle as those you are "ready and willing to do a big favor for at a moment's notice."

If you took some time, you could probably make some interesting lists of people comprising your inner circle and your social circle. Your social circle might have a couple dozen friends from school, in your neighborhood, on your sports teams and so on. I'm not saying you have to actually do this exercise and start voting people in or out of your tribe, but the concept of having an inner circle and a social circle are very important to consider. This is particularly true today, in the age of social media, when you have the potential to interact with too many friends.

You might be thinking, "But Leslie, I have a ton of friends—1,179 to be exact!" Let me guess, are we talking about Facebook? I'm sure you have loads of friends online and endless interactions involving them, but those (for the most part) don't actually count as authentic friendships. Sit and think—how many of those friends do you actually spend face-to-face time with regularly? How many of them would you drop everything for and spend the whole weekend helping to recover from wisdom tooth surgery? The friends you really do interact with and do mutual favors for in real life are part of your inner circle—your wolf pack! The others, the ones based in social media, can actually become distractions that compromise the quality of your inner and social circle relationships.

Don't get me wrong. I have some friends online that I have had many conversations with and care about, regardless of never having actually met them in real life. It can be really neat to grow your network beyond your town or state, past your country or even your continent. But remember, the interactions you have with these people account for hours spent behind a computer screen and cause you to miss out on real human interaction. Like seeing someone's facial expression as they tell you a funny joke, the impact of human touch when you hug a loved one hello, or the sense of community when you do things together. We are hardwired for these real life human encounters, and you're selling yourself short when you eliminate those aspects from your life.

Setting Your Motivation into Motion

Mood and mindset matter more than you might realize. Think of it this way: if you need to turn in an essay for English class first thing tomorrow morning, or else you'll get an F and your parents won't let you go to the high school football game Friday night, what mood is the best to help you finish?

- Mood #1: mad. You're so mad that you have to finish this paper to go to the game because all of your friends already got permission to go from their parents.

- Mood #2: nervous. You're really nervous about getting a good grade on the essay, because if you get a C, your parents might not let you go to the next big game.

- Mood #3: excited. You're actually really excited to do the research required for the essay because you like the topic, and you're excited about the big game Friday.

Feeling mad or nervous is going to hinder the research and thought required for the project. If you're excited, that paper is going to be done in no time, not to mention you'll probably enjoy yourself! This is all thanks to a positive mindset. But what do you do if you feel like moods #1 or #2 and you realize you need to feel like #3 to accomplish the task? The answer is easier than you think: decide to change your mood to change your mindset!

To switch gears and put yourself into a better mental space, first you need to figure out what mental space you want to be in. To do this, look at your current situation and the desired end result. Let's say your team is playing a volleyball game tonight after school and you feel annoyed about the game because you'd much rather watch the VMA's tonight with your other girlfriends who aren't on the team. It'd be easy to blow the game off, but you've also worked really hard all season and just want to have a good time and win! This means your current situation is the game, and your desired outcome is to have fun and win.

Take a moment and realize that you're annoyed. That's okay. Accept it, but keep the bigger goal in sight. Maybe you can TiVo the awards show and watch it with your friends tomorrow—which would leave them open to be invited to your game! With the support of your friends at your game, you can have fun and help lead your team to victory. Mood + Mindset = Success.

What if changing your mood is proving to be more difficult than clicking your heels together three times and making a wish? Here are some helpful tips to direct you in a different direction:

- Know exactly what it is that you need from a situation, like getting your essay finished to go to the game.

- Listen to music that excites you to get down to business.

- If you need to knock this paper out, change your setting to one that will be more conducive to concentration.

- If you've been sitting at a dark desk for too long, switch it up. Stand and write, or just go for a refreshing walk around the block to help you out of your rut.

- If you need a research buddy, seek the help of someone who will encourage and boost you, not slow you down.

- Encourage yourself with positive affirmations, and channel that cheering you can't wait to hear at the game Friday night.

Now that you've got your mood and mindset on point, motivation should start trickling in. You're on top of the world and feel like you can do anything! How else can you take these new skills and apply them to other aspects of your life? Do you want to get in really good shape by the spring dance? Do you want to kick some serious butt at next week's game? Do you want to start having more fun? Then it's time that you set some serious goals for yourself. Get a calendar and start filling it in with all the things that you want to do. Of course, give yourself ample time for goals that are going to take a bit longer, like building muscle or losing weight. When you have a positive mindset and the tools you need to accomplish your goals, the world is your playground.

What if your goals are too big or seem too far off and you find yourself losing motivation? Pencil in some rewards on your calendar! If it's going to take six weeks to get in shape for baseball season, break those six weeks down into two-week interim goals. For example:

- Goal #1: weeks one and two. Slow introduction to light weight training, easy cardio, and stretching.

- Goal #2: weeks three and four. Increased weight training, moderate cardio, and stretching.

- Goal #3: weeks five and six. Max weight training, "game-pace" cardio, and stretching.

By breaking your goals down to smaller fragments in time, you don't get so caught up in training at game pace for six weeks straight. And you get to celebrate each time you achieve a mini-goal! For example, your rewards may go a little something like this:

> • Goal #1: a new baseball hat.
>
> • Goal #2: a new baseball glove.
>
> • Goal #3: Dad will take you to a pro baseball game.

So you've mastered the art of feeling good and being motivated; what's left to do? It's time to pay it forward! Paying it forward means to pay a good deed back to others, as opposed to the original person who helped you. In this case, my words and this book have helped you blossom and become one serious kick-butt Primal teen girl. Now it's your turn to pay it forward and help the people you love and care about the most. It doesn't have to be another girl your age—it could be guys in your class, younger kids in your neighborhood, your parents, or any other individuals in your life that you think could benefit from the wisdom you now hold.

Not only does giving back make you feel good about yourself, but it's also good for your health. It's been shown that people who volunteer have lower levels of stress, inflammation, and cholesterol. Not to mention, helping others also helps you get out of your own head and elude the awful "self-chatter" that tends to eat away at you when left idle for too long. It helps you be in the moment. It helps you gain confidence. It helps you be a part of a community. What's more Primal than that?

The question now is, "How are you going to pay it forward?"

Chapter Five: At a Glance

If Your Family Freaks
There are a number of reasons your family might not agree with your new Primal lifestyle. They might not understand what being paleo is all about, they simply might not agree with it, they could think it's too expensive, or it could be against their religious beliefs. Whatever the problem, the key is communication. Discuss why you want to live a paleo lifestyle and you just might even get them on board too!

How to Deal
Bullies are not cool, but there are some actions you can take to stand up to them. In an attempt to try and impress those around you, peer pressure can force you into doing things that you wouldn't normally do. Most times people associate peer pressure with negative actions, but sometimes it has a positive push. Self-esteem is all about how you feel about yourself, and is often tied to your personal body image. Teens with poor self-esteem can sometimes fall victim to things like bullies and peer pressure because they don't feel strong enough to stand up for themselves. Sometimes these teens can even fall victim to eating disorders such as anorexia or bulimia. Eating disorders are a real illness and if you or someone you know is suffering from one, seek professional help.

Your Wolf Pack
Because of social media, the landscape of our inner and social circles has changed quite drastically from Grokette's social environment 10,000 years ago. For your hunter-gather ancestors, an inner circle consisted of about a dozen close friends and family. Outside of that was a social circle of approximately 25 people. These people were all part of a community that looked out for each other. Today, you can have an endless number of friends and relationships set in a digital world, and might, consequently, be missing out on genuine, one-on-one connections.

Setting your Motivation into Motion
One of the easiest ways to become motivated is to change your mood and your mindset. When you're happy and positive, great things happen for you—as opposed to someone who is grumpy and negative all the time and nothing ever seems to go her way. Once you become a master of motivation, pay it forward and spread the joy to those around you.

Chapter Six

Success 101: Nailed It!

Congratulations!

You've made it to the end of *Paleo Girl* and are fully armed with every bit of knowledge you need to take on the world! And while this insight will help you along your way, sometimes it's beneficial to learn from other girls just like you. What do your peers look to achieve when going Primal? What about the paleo journey has been hard for them? What do they eat? Who are their biggest cheerleaders along the way? Sometimes a girl just needs some real-world examples—and that's exactly what this chapter is all about. Consider this exclusive access into the diaries of seven girls who have stood in the exact spot you stand in right now.

Learn from these dedicated and courageous teens who want to pay it forward and help you. Once you're ready to embark on your Primal journey, keep track of your very own story and use it to help others or just to reflect on all of your amazing efforts. Sometimes seeing how far you've come is the exact motivation you need to cross the finish line.

Erin Beacham

What goals were you looking to accomplish when going Primal?

I got really interested in science (especially biology) in high school, and I began reading about nutrition online. I didn't have specific goals other than wanting to eat and live in a way that my body was designed for.

How successful were you in sticking with your plan?

Overall, I'm very successful in sticking with Primal. I'm currently in college, and I chose this year to not have a meal plan. I cook entirely for myself, using the best quality ingredients I can find. I'm lucky in that I don't have to worry too much about sticking to a budget, so I'm able to take advantage of locally grown and organic food in my area (Philadelphia). I definitely go with the 80/20 rule though to still enjoy some parts of this time in my life I wouldn't experience otherwise.

What were your biggest hurdles, and how did you overcome them?

During a period in high school, I became overly concerned with the "goodness" of my diet. I ate too few calories and lost an unhealthy amount of weight, which has been difficult to recover from.

What was your biggest accomplishment?

I got into my dream school! I'm currently studying bioengineering at the University of Pennsylvania.

What does your average daily meal plan consist of?

Breakfast is usually two or three eggs with onions stir-fried in butter and maybe some kale, or a banana with almond butter, honey, and cinnamon if I need the carbs. Lunches and dinners are often very similar—I pick a type of meat and a vegetable and go from there. My favorite meal is duck breast with asparagus roasted in the leftover duck fat. Occasionally I'll add in squash, sweet potatoes,

or wild rice if I need extra carbs. Snacks are pistachios and sometimes other nuts, dark chocolate, and if I didn't have it for breakfast, a banana with almond butter.

What does your average weekly exercise routine consist of?
I do CrossFit two or three times weekly and am part of the running club. We compete in cross-country races in the fall and track races in the spring.

Beyond going Primal, what's the hardest part about being a teenager?
The stress of school, definitely. In high school I was extremely concerned with doing well in all my classes—most of them honors or AP. I also played French horn in marching band, concert band, and a local community band, which took up about 20 additional hours a week. Senior year, I thought I would collapse under the pressure of college applications. Now that I'm in college, the stress of schoolwork continues to be an issue I struggle with on a daily basis. I hear a lot about the importance of "leaving work at work," but with school, you can't really do that.

What's your support system like?
My parents neither supported nor resisted my efforts to live Primal, as we have an emotionally detached relationship. My friends were also never very concerned with my diet, but they did think it was strange I bragged about eating a high-fat diet.

Is there anything your support system would like to say?
I really didn't have any advocates on this journey—I'm essentially self-motivated.

Is there anything else you want teens like you to know about going Primal?
It can be done, and it feels so much better than eating crap and living like crap.

Katrina Bohnhorst

What goals were you looking to accomplish when going Primal?

I didn't know what to expect. In winter of my sophomore year of college, I cut out grains for a day to see if it would remove my excessive flatulence and bloating. Needless to say, it definitely did. Gradually, I was able to remove dairy and that made me realize how intolerant I was to both grains and dairy. Removing those foods completely also alleviated my anxiety, which I started to get a bad case of. After finally being 100 percent paleo for a few months, I noticed my resistance to carbs and sugar. So I started to lower my daily intake of net carbs. At first 150, then 100, 75, 60, 50, and now it's around 30 per day. I only reduced the amount because my body was not handling carbs that well. I would experience sugar highs and then sugar lows and I didn't like how unstable my mood/energy would be from consuming carbs. Basically, the longer I stayed paleo, the more sensitive my body became to many substances. But, with the carb intake that I'm now doing, I have definitely noticed an optimal health for myself. Again, everyone is different and can handle certain foods differently, but this is what worked and is still working for me.

How successful were you in sticking with your plan?

Once I knew that grains were one of the culprits with my digestive/energy issues, it gave me motivation to stick to being grain free. It was difficult because at the time I was experiencing over-training with college athletics and stress from school so it led to countless sugar cravings. I did cave many times, but after a few months I decided to completely cut out dairy, and with no grains and no dairy, as well as cutting out chronic cardio, I did eliminate those sugar cravings. With no sugar cravings, paleo and keto are rather easy for me to stick to. Also, with no cravings I can enjoy baking allergy friendly treats for myself and still have great digestion and mood.

What were your biggest hurdles, and how did you overcome them?
Overcoming the sugar binges was my toughest hurdle. I would be 100 percent paleo except for the sugar binges, which were on cookies, ice cream, brownies, and cake...whatever was around. It got to the point where I was fed up with how those binges affected my life and how my anxiety levels were getting worse and worse. I chose to take care of myself and to respect myself and that's what ultimately helped me conquer the binging.

What was your biggest accomplishment?
My biggest accomplishment has to be making it this far in my journey. I listen to my body and do things for myself regardless of others' opinions. I finally eliminated the binging, which has helped me live with a healthy mind and body.

What does your average daily meal plan consist of?
For breakfast I love to eat eggs and bacon. I really don't know how I haven't gotten sick of bacon yet for how much of it I eat, but anyways that is just a staple breakfast every day. For lunch, I typically will eat some sort of meat (chicken, pork, beef) with some guacamole or sauce. As snacks, I will eat almond butter with shredded coconut, berries, or any paleo/keto treat. I don't typically eat mid-afternoon and evenings because I'm just not hungry and I make sure to eat breakfast, lunch, and a couple snacks to get enough nutrition in. If I'm hungry I eat, and during dinnertime I just don't get any desire to eat.

What does your average weekly exercise routine consist of?
I am a tennis player and runner. I typically play tennis three or four days a week, or run three and four days a week. I either do one or the other, not both. If I run, I'll run between two or three miles, and I go for speed. For tennis, I typically hit for 30 or 60 minutes. I work out to feel good, not to strain myself.

What's your support system like?
Honestly, the only support I had was myself. Everyone I know eats the Standard American Diet and doesn't really see how I can possibly not tolerate grains or dairy. That never made the transition easy, but I was determined to take care of my digestive and emotional troubles. I do research daily on fitness/health and I've found what is best for me. Only recently did I even open up to my family about my food allergies and this whole health journey since I'm in college hours from home.

Is there anything your support system would like to say?
I'm finally happy, both mind and body and I did it by myself (with the help of research of course). No one motivated me or told me what to do. It was a personal journey that has led to only great things.

Is there anything else you want teens like you to know about going Primal?
I firmly believe that everyone should live a Primal life. Since I am intolerant to dairy I consider myself paleo and keto. But, I think that everyone should go Primal and see the benefits for themselves. Everyone is different, so my benefits may be slightly different from someone else's, but my life has improved so much from this transition. I believe that others should be able to experience the best life imaginable and going Primal can contribute to that.

Monica Bravo

What goals were you looking to accomplish when going Primal?

My story began during my sophomore/junior year of high school. I had terrible digestion issues (constipation) and I wanted to lose 10 pounds. I am a ballerina, and my weight would fluctuate five or six pounds every day. I counted calories and did whatever I could to get the weight where I needed for performances. I didn't have much of a concern for my health, until my father, a former triathlete, was found to have blockages to his heart. Our Primal journey began together, after he realized the SAD diet had brought him to a hospital. And, although exercise may have prevented him from a fatal heart attack, it wasn't enough to keep him healthy. This life-changing event brought me to dig deep into the definition of health.

We found *The Primal Blueprint* together and have been MDA readers for three years now. Although at first my goals were to lose weight, which did happen, and solve my stomach issues, which also happened, my goals now are tremendously different. Today I write a blog (bravoforpaleo.com) and try to inspire young people to eat better and go Primal too!

How successful were you in sticking with your plan?

It took me about 8 to 12 months to fully transition into a strict regimen, with no "cheating." It wasn't until I found my true motivation, that I could be 95 or 100 percent Primal. Once I realized I wanted to lead by example and be a role model, then it became easy to stay strict, and my results were drastic. I had to give up my obsession with calories and my fear of fat before I could get there. I have been fully Primal for a year and a half now.

What were your biggest hurdles, and how did you overcome them?
It was pivotal that I had a paradigm shift, and sometimes that is not easy. Especially when you are surrounded by teenage girls complaining about every inch of fat and starving themselves. I had to change my relationship with food to get where I am today. I overcame my problems by taking it day by day and reminding myself of the bigger picture, my health and happiness. Although 90 percent of my peers didn't care or want to care about their health, I realized it was okay to be different and they'll follow eventually. Things worked out and now people ask me about Primal eating every day! All of my friends who thought I was "weird" for not eating pizza, now are interested in the Primal lifestyle too.

What was your biggest accomplishment?
My biggest accomplishment was launching my blog three months ago. I could name 100 other amazing things that came along with eating Primal, but being able to share it with people my age has been amazing. During my journey, I think my biggest accomplishment was when I got to the point where food was fuel and no longer the enemy.

What does your average daily meal plan consist of?
It varies depending on what is available at the farmers market, and what my body "needs,"...but typically...Breakfast: eggs, with meat (bacon or sausage from the farmers market), and spinach and onions. Lunch: usually doesn't happen...maybe an apple and almond butter or some leftover dinner or a salad with homemade dressing. Dinner: grass-fed beef, chicken, or turkey...you name it, with at least two servings of vegetables. Other miscellaneous: fruit, sweet potatoes, kombucha tea, 90-percent dark chocolate, red wine—these all depend on my activity level and my goals at that time.

What does your average weekly exercise routine consist of?
For the first five months I was dancing three to four hours a day, five days a week. Then I stopped taking ballet classes (when I got to college), and I began CrossFit, weight lifting, yoga, and walking.

Beyond going Primal, what's the hardest part about being a teenager?
Peer pressure. When you're a teenager, you're not really sure about who you are yet. It's a constant struggle to find yourself and learn how to express yourself confidently. People will pressure you to be certain ways and fit a mold, and you aren't sure where you fit yet. It's a time of learning, and so it can be hard when you make mistakes and have to learn from them.

What's your support system like?
My family is a wonderful support system. My mom is my cheerleader and my dad is a leader. My best friends support me in everything I do and motivate me to be a better person. I have a health coach named John Reilly, who first suggested that I join my dad and go gluten and dairy free. He saw me at my worst (when I couldn't even look in the mirror) and brought me to my best.

Is there anything your support system would like to say?
My best friend Elizabeth says, "I support Monica in every way! I think the biggest thing I have to do sometimes is just to listen and encourage! I remind her of her bigger goals and not to sweat the small stuff."

Is there anything else you want teens like you to know about going Primal?
I want them to know it's possible. Most of them think they could never give up bread and pizza and other junk food, but they CAN and they'll feel so much better. I think it's important for them to educate themselves about what's healthy and what's not, because we're the future. We're the future doctors, dieticians, parents, educators, etc. And we can change the way society views food.

Christy Carfagno

What goals were you looking to accomplish when going Primal?

I first discovered the paleo diet on Easter during my junior year in high school. I was a three-sport varsity athlete; playing tennis, running track, and starting my first season of lacrosse, so I was constantly looking for foods to fuel my performance and give me energy. I'd been "dieting" for about three years, focusing more on being skinny than strong but was always able to stay competitive in my sport. When I saw *The Paleo Diet for Athletes* on a shelf in Athleta, I immediately grabbed it and was intrigued. Eating as we were designed to made complete sense to me, and the more I learned, the more I began to shift towards eating to live and grow rather than to become skinny.

How successful were you in sticking with your plan?

Paleo has changed my life completely. I started when I was 17; I'm now 19 and a freshman in college. When I began I ate relatively strict paleo, maybe a treat once a week such as a slice of pizza, but I ate plenty of eggs, chicken, salad, fruit, nuts, and dates. I went very strict paleo entering my senior year for tennis preseason. I went on and off after the season, but discovered how sick I felt eating non-paleo foods, so I now eat strict paleo. I'd say I'm 100 percent, with maybe a small treat every two weeks or once a month. I feel best when I eat this way and don't feel the desire to binge or give in to temptation when I'm with my friends.

What were your biggest hurdles, and how did you overcome them?

I've had more than a few bumps in the road with paleo. Once I became a senior, I began partying and letting loose with my friends, which was a change for me. I'd always had fun but focused on grades and fitness first. The lax in schoolwork carried over to my diet and exercise regimen, and I began treating myself, binging, and even tried going a week back on the SAD, which made me so sick I got a stomach bug for three days. I was searching for a way to have fun and be "normal" but my back and forth dieting continued to make me sick and I continued to gain weight. Despite this hard time, I refused to give up. I knew paleo wasn't the problem; it had been so good to me for an entire year and the concepts made so much sense. I tweaked my diet by adding more protein and more carbs (I had gone incredibly low carb earlier) and started eating more intuitively. My energy returned and cravings reduced, and I began working out to build strength rather than endurance.

What was your biggest accomplishment?
My biggest accomplishment has been managing to stay 100 percent paleo in college. No, I don't know where the school's chicken is from and I don't know if the beef is grass fed, but that's not the point. I feel great, my workouts are better than ever, and I'm able to eat delicious food consistently without feeling the need for more. I've started a blog and an Instagram that monitors my college paleo life, and I've had tons of classmates follow me and ask me questions. I advocate, I educate, and I exemplify the paleo lifestyle to the best of my abilities. While I'm not perfect by any means, I do understand the greater meaning of paleo and that it's so much more than a diet. My friends joke about my "all natural" lifestyle but I don't mind living the caveman life here on campus :)

What does your average daily meal plan consist of?
Breakfast: two hardboiled eggs, 1 ounce almonds, black coffee. Post workout: one medium baked sweet potato, 4 ounces grilled chicken. Lunch: 6-8 ounces grilled chicken, 2-3 cups steamed/roasted veggies. Snack: one small apple, 1 ounce almonds. Dinner: 6-8 ounces protein (varies nightly), 2-3 cups veggies. Nightly: tea with chia seeds mixed in.

What does your average weekly exercise routine consist of?
Sunday: legs; Monday: chest/arms; Tuesday: shoulders/back; Wednesday: HIIT cardio; Thursday: Circuit training; Friday/Saturday: rest days.

Beyond going Primal, what's the hardest part about being a teenager?
Emotion. I'm not talking about hormones, but nerves about school, work, social life, family, boyfriends, leaving home, sports, EVERYTHING can be so stressful if not managed well. I've had to deal with all of these things at some point and they can complicate everything from diet to exercise to energy. What I've found most

important is to keep your mindset positive through any of these stressors. Finding the good in any situation and always finding an excuse to laugh has gotten me through so many hard times, and although it sounds simple, I believe appreciating the little things can make life 100 percent more enjoyable.

What's your support system like?
My friends have been my biggest support. My mom's a wonderful cook and still gets upset when I don't eat her pasta salad or rice pilaf, but my family supports me all the same. My friends provide me with the real enthusiasm about diet and exercise that I can feed off constantly. They make it easy and fun to go out and eat what I want without feeling judged.

Is there anything your support system would like to say?
From my friend: "I consider Christy an inspiration. I follow her Instagram Primalteen and love seeing what she eats every day and what workout she's doing. It takes such willpower to stay consistent in college, but she makes it seem easy!"

Is there anything else you want teens like you to know about going Primal?
Do your thing. What other people think of your lifestyle is none of your concern; if people hold you back or bring you down, meet new ones, and always respect yourself enough to live the way that makes YOU feel best. No one else is inside your head, no one knows how you feel when you eat a certain way or when you workout. Live to feel good and live to grow. Discover new things and keep an open mind because you never know what you can learn from anyone else. Listen to your body and most important—don't beat yourself up over slip-ups! They're in the past; learn from them and improve the next day.

Riley Madrian

What goals were you looking to accomplish when going Primal?
My goal was to be healthier from the inside out. The Mark's Daily Apple website was recommended to me by a teacher of mine when I told her I had been dealing with a stomach ulcer for two weeks. She told me ulcers are often a result of a poor diet. I had never given my diet much thought but I knew something had to change. Why not start with what I put in my body? I visited the MDA website and I was reading article after article for hours on end! Everything made so much sense. I also read many success stories and figured, "If they can do it, why not me?"

How successful were you in sticking with your plan?
When I commit to something, it is all or nothing. Therefore, once I decided to go Primal, it was easy for me to stick to it. It also helped that the Primal lifestyle is very simple to follow. My parents were also starting the South Beach diet at the same time, so I had more low-carb foods available to me. Even so, when I did eat school lunch, I'd often have to leave most of it uneaten. Fries? Chocolate milk? Garlic bread? No, thank you! I would just eat my salad and wait until I got home to have something more satiating. Through all the weird looks and annoying comments, it was worth it.

What were your biggest hurdles, and how did you overcome them?
I had a hard time implementing an exercise program. I didn't really exercise unless encouraged by my parents. Once I started to lose weight, I was able to see more muscle definition in my legs, and, like a total girl, I wanted to make them look better. So I started doing squats and calf raises, and I liked what I saw. My

mom would comment on how great my legs were looking and that motivated me even more. Pretty soon, I also noticed how I felt even better (if that was even possible) when I exercised. Before I knew it, I had overcome what had once stressed me out.

What was your biggest accomplishment?
My biggest accomplishment is my consistent happiness and energy throughout the day. When I used to crash from my high-carb "healthy" breakfast, I am now energized and able to focus on learning. I am often amazed at how my friends complain every day about being tired and hungry, yet instead of being proactive (or even reactive), they slug through every day accepting low energy as the norm. Nothing feels better than having energy and passion for things in life.

What does your average daily meal plan consist of?
I eat three or four eggs (scrambled) for breakfast, and about once a week, I also have a fruit smoothie with protein powder. I pack a snack bag of mixed nuts if I'm hungry before lunch. Then I pack a Big A** Salad for lunch. I always look forward to my big salad. Depending on what we had for dinner the night before, I might throw leftover meat on it too. Then, for dinner I eat what my mom made for the family. I try to help with the making of dinner so that I can use butter or olive oil instead of vegetable oil, or add more veggies to the meal. Then, if I'm hungry before bed I eat a boiled egg.

What does your average weekly exercise routine consist of?
I do the Primal Essential Movements about once a week, and continue to progress through the levels. I loved sprinting once I tried it (as an exercise; I have sprinted before) so I sprint about twice a week. Other than that, I just try to walk more. I take the stairs or take the long way to class. I also play outside more on Saturdays, which I guess is technically exercise.

Beyond going Primal, what's the hardest part about being a teenager?
Balancing everything! Homework, practicing violin, family time, friend time, and personal health are a lot to deal with. I also find it hard to see myself as a separate entity from my parents. I have many of the same opinions, but also many different ones. How do I voice mine without disrespecting theirs? Do I even know what I believe? I often need to just sit and think about how I want to live my life, especially because once I go off to college and live on my own, I will have to

make decisions for me and me alone. How do I know I will make the right ones? Making big life decisions is what I find to be the hardest part of being a teenager.

What's your support system like?
Outside of my family, I don't really have a support system. My friends just consider me the "healthy" friend, but leave it at that. My family on the other hand, is a great support system. They don't really ask very much about what being Primal means beyond the basics. They support me in what I want, unless they think they know better. I can't ask for much better, but sometimes I just want to scream to them, "Real bacon is not bad for you!" (They are fans of turkey bacon. Ew.)

Is there anything your support system would like to say?
My mom says, "I have been extremely impressed by Riley's dedication and discipline when it comes to following her Primal diet and exercise routine. We have gone through the first two phases of the South Beach diet and when we have struggled, Riley has stayed strong. I also like how she is flexible enough with guests and others to not make her diet be an awkward issue."

Is there anything else you want teens like you to know about going Primal?
It's not as hard as it seems! Do whatever you need to go Primal. It is the best way to live and feel better about life in general. Also, if you can't find a good support system, the MDA forum is a great place to go if you have questions or need help. The best way to deal with people or parents that question your diet changes is to be an example and show them how great it is to live Primal.

Mallory Osugi

What goals were you looking to accomplish when going Primal?
I wanted to lose unhealthy fat, gain muscle, minimize my toxin exposure, and live the way a human being is meant to live. I feel that it is wrong that disease and sickness are such a normal part of life, and I thought maybe I could touch the optimal, rather than living the toxic lifestyle America calls "normal."

How successful were you in sticking with your plan?
I succeeded easily. Of course, I had hurdles, but knowing the alternative was shoving my body towards death and disease made the choices easy.

What were your biggest hurdles, and how did you overcome them?
The biggest hurdle may have been the social aspect—eating an extraordinarily different diet from everyone around me, including my friends and family. Some people just can't imagine why anyone would, under no circumstances, eat a donut. To them, everything, (including donuts) is acceptable in moderation. In the end, however, I learned to respect the choices of others, and, with the motive of their well-being in mind, occasionally (and gently) steer them in the right direction. Another hurdle was budgeting, but you really save on other things (like prescription and over-the-counter drugs, which I once relied upon), and over time I found great sources of fairly inexpensive, quality food. One large hurdle was learning to eat optimally at restaurants, and at school on a meal plan. But working the system wasn't too difficult, and a few letters to the school helped more healthful options become available.

What was your biggest accomplishment?
My biggest accomplishment was losing 20 pounds, all while feeling strong and healthy, and maintaining what was important in my life, like my relationships, despite the drastic change.

What does your average daily meal plan consist of?
Breakfasts are typically a few eggs, and cup of veggies sautéed in some grass-fed and finished tallow. Lunch is the jumbo (large-derriere) salad, leafy greens and broccoli and various veggies, a spoonful of quality olive oil and vinegar, and a portion of chicken, or other meat. Dinner is meat again; maybe steak, and a large side of veggies like Brussels sprouts, with more fat. Yum!

What does your average weekly exercise routine consist of?
I walk several miles a day, and intersperse short exercises throughout my day, like planks and pushups, after, say, sitting and doing homework for half an hour.

Beyond going Primal, what's the hardest part about being a teenager?
The hardest part of being a teenager is adapting in general—change is hard. Believing in what I'm doing makes the change worth it, and much more bearable!

What's your support system like?
My family was at first scornful, but as they realized I knew my stuff (thanks MDA!), they grew to respect my decision and began supporting me more and more. They even made similar changes in their lives.

Is there anything your support system would like to say?
From my mom: "She seemed to be on some crazy diet, but it only took some time to realize it was actually doing some good. Since she began, we have gardened together, gone to the farmers market together, and it has been a bonding and enjoyable experience."

Is there anything else you want teens like you to know about going Primal?
Believe in what you're doing. Don't stress, have fun with it, and take baby steps if you need to. Just don't seek out arguments with those who don't eat the way you believe they should—have some tact and respect!

Sarah Tognoli

What goals were you looking to accomplish when going Primal?
To find something to give me a new sense of hope. Going Primal, for me, was a process. As an adolescent, you get this idea in your head of how everything is supposed to go, how you're supposed to look, what you're supposed to achieve, and how you're supposed to feel, and when the reality hits that life has very different plans in mind for you, it can really take a toll on you mentally and physically.

How successful were you in sticking with your plan?
Success did not come on the first try, or the second, or the third for that matter. I failed and picked myself back up many times throughout this journey, but each time I chose to move forward instead of giving up, I felt this sense of power that pushed me on. I did not let myself feel weak for getting sidetracked; instead, I decided to take something from each incident and learn from it. My 'plan' changed a million times throughout the process, but throughout the ups and downs I felt myself getting stronger, and more in tune with my body.

What were your biggest hurdles, and how did you overcome them?
I struggled with many things during my journey to becoming Primal, the first transitioning months being the most difficult. There were times when I felt deprived and frustrated. From feeling completely limited on the things that I could eat to spending time with friends who had not a care in the world about their health, the simplest things in my life suddenly became complicated. The first thing I did in an attempt to counteract these new concerns was to teach myself how to cook. I took a silent vow to eat whatever my heart desired, without breaking the boundaries of my newly adapted lifestyle.

After quickly getting a grip in the kitchen, I moved on to the gym. My progress was slow and difficult at first. I felt like I was running in place, literally. I kept going though, not letting anything be an excuse for me not to. The hardships only lasted about a month. Soon I started seeing results and getting stronger than I had ever been before. I stopped going out with friends for a few weeks to really let myself focus on making the initial change, and when I felt comfortable enough, I began to incorporate my social life into my new Primal ways. My friends and extended family thought some of the things that I did were strange at first, but quickly adapted and I became Sarah "The Primal One," which I was perfectly content with. I felt incredible, and to me, that was all that mattered.

What was your biggest accomplishment?
I've gained so many things throughout this journey, but the biggest for me is rather an array of small things accumulated into one great accomplishment. The sense of power I feel when I'm outside running or in the gym lifting, that push that tells me I can make it for one more mile or lift that last rep. When family, friends, peers, coworkers, and even strangers tell me how much I've inspired them. When I feel the support of my loved ones as they travel with me through this Primal journey. When I see my sense of commitment to this lifestyle seep into other areas of my life and cause me to work harder and go farther than I ever have before. Finally, it's being truly content with my body for the first time in my life after years spent battling with self-confidence. I feel proud to have accomplished something so big that it has literally changed my life in just about every aspect, and has brought me more positive outcomes than I could have ever imagined. That is by far my biggest accomplishment.

What does your average daily meal plan consist of?
While losing my initial 20-25 pounds eating Primal, I never once counted my calories or really monitored my food intake at all. The one simple meal plan rule I did follow was eating exactly what I wanted every single day, as long as it fit within my new lifestyle. I start the day with three or four eggs, a few slices of bacon, and whatever fruit I feel like eating that day, switching it up with paleo pancakes and waffles throughout the week. I snack on nuts and berries throughout the afternoon and have a salad topped with fruits or vegetables and some sort of protein source, nuts, chicken, or even steak, or I have a turkey sandwich on two slices of homemade Primal bread for lunch.

After another light meal in the afternoon, usually consisting of whatever is left-over from dinner the night before, I cook dinner. I try to keep a bit of variety in my diet so dinner is different every night. Salmon with baked sweet potatoes, roasted chicken with artichokes, and seared pork loins with sautéed apples are a few examples. I also make room for dessert at least a few times a week, ranging from "Apple Crisp" from elanaspantry.com to a more simple "Cake in a Mug" from paleomg.com.

What does your average weekly exercise routine consist of?
My average weekly exercise routine started out with going to the gym three to four days a week and running a mile or two on the treadmill. It was simple and it wasn't easy, but I felt proud for going and soon it became second nature. I noticed myself being able to run farther and farther, and within a few months I could run five miles without much hesitation. After a leg injury that kept me from running for a while, I reluctantly decided to start some weight training to keep myself active. Two weeks of weight lifting and I was hooked. I became addicted to that feeling when I mustered up all of my strength and somehow pumped out the last rep of my set. And, of course, waking up the next day sore as ever from my efforts.

Soon, I saw my body begin to change into something that I had never been before, an athlete. I even started running again when I could and became more active outside of the gym by biking and hiking whenever the opportunity came around. I now weight train six days a week along with a variety of cardio whenever I feel like it, and I couldn't be happier!

Beyond going Primal, what's the hardest part about being a teenager?
Simply struggling to figure everything out. For the first time, I am the one calling the shots in my life and making decisions for myself. As much as everyone tried to prepare me for being an adult, it still is a huge transition. There are days when I feel pressure to have everything figured out for myself, and times when I wonder if I'm doing anything right. I do my best to have a positive attitude though, and continue to push forward, figuring out the

details along the way. There are more good days than there are bad, and I have learned so many things through each experience that I'm slowly beginning to feel more comfortable on my own.

Is there anything your support system would like to say?
I asked my mother if she would write this paragraph for me, and this is what she sent: "What matters most is how far you've come. You did have a lot of support and love but you alone made these choices to stick with it and keep going every day even when you got sidetracked. You made the choice to go this way and look where you are in just a matter of months! I am so proud of you and I can't wait to see where you go now!"

Is there anything else you want teens like you to know about going Primal?
There may be times when you feel like the odd girl out, and I guarantee that you will have people at some point try to tell you that what you're doing is wrong or even ridiculous. Don't worry about what anyone else is doing; if going Primal feels right to you, do it. Don't let anything stop you. Age, race, genetics, gender, whatever it may be, it is irrelevant to becoming the best that you can be.

Your Personal Journal

Now it's time for the fun part! This is your opportunity to track your progress, reflect upon your struggles, and share your story with others. Use this space for you. You'll learn a ton from yourself, and you can share it with friends and family members when you've reached your goals. Be a shining example, and pay it forward!

Name: _____

Age: _____

Date: _____

What goals were you looking to accomplish when going Primal?

_____
_____
_____
_____
_____
_____
_____
_____
_____
_____
_____
_____
_____
_____
_____
_____
_____

How successful were you in sticking with your plan?

_____
_____
_____
_____
_____
_____
_____
_____
_____
_____
_____
_____
_____
_____

What were your biggest hurdles, and how did you overcome them?

_____
_____
_____
_____
_____
_____
_____
_____
_____
_____
_____
_____
_____
_____

What was your biggest accomplishment?

_____
_____
_____
_____
_____
_____
_____
_____
_____
_____
_____
_____

What does your average daily meal plan consist of?

_____
_____
_____
_____
_____
_____
_____
_____
_____
_____
_____
_____
_____
_____
_____

What does your average weekly exercise routine consist of?

_____
_____
_____
_____
_____
_____
_____
_____
_____
_____
_____
_____
_____
_____
_____
_____
_____
_____

Beyond going Primal, what's the hardest part about being a teenager?

_____
_____
_____
_____
_____
_____
_____
_____
_____
_____
_____
_____
_____
_____
_____
_____

What's your support system like?

_____
_____
_____
_____
_____
_____
_____
_____
_____
_____
_____
_____
_____
_____
_____

Is there anything your support system would like to say?

_____
_____
_____
_____
_____
_____
_____
_____
_____
_____
_____
_____
_____
_____

Is there anything else you want teens like you to know about going Primal?

_____
_____
_____
_____
_____
_____
_____
_____
_____
_____
_____
_____
_____
_____
_____

Notes:

_____
_____
_____
_____
_____
_____
_____
_____
_____
_____
_____
_____
_____
_____
_____
_____
_____

Before Photo and Date

After Photo and Date:

DIY 101: Let's Make It!

New to the Kitchen?

Whether you're a master chef or you don't even know where the kitchen is located in your house, here's a brief introduction to some of the measurements and terms you'll find in this chapter so you can DIY—do it yourself!

Measurements

- Pinch: think about literally using your fingertips to grab a pinch of a dry ingredient. Typically $\frac{1}{16}$ teaspoon.

- Dash: also for dry ingredients, this is slightly more than a pinch. Typically $\frac{1}{8}$ teaspoon.

- Splash: this measurement is for liquid ingredients and is typically anywhere between $\frac{1}{8}$ and $\frac{1}{32}$ of an ounce.

- Handful: literally the amount you can hold in your hand. Although this measurement can vary, it's roughly between $\frac{1}{3}$ and $\frac{1}{2}$ cup.

- Dollop: think about taking a scoop of a semi-liquid condiment and plopping it on your plate. Typically a "heaping tablespoon" or a little more than a tablespoon.

- lb: an abbreviation for pound.

- oz: an abbreviation for ounce.

- tbsp: an abbreviation for tablespoon.

- tsp: an abbreviation for teaspoon.

Terms

- Dice: to cut food into small ½ or ¼ inch cubes.

- Roughly cut: not precisely cut, but randomly cut. You'll see this when the shape of the food doesn't matter or doesn't alter the outcome of the dish.

- To taste: this expression is used most often when it comes to salt and pepper or other spices. It's your own preference for the amount of seasoning in a dish.

- Bite-sized: small enough of a size to comfortably pop in your mouth all at once.

- Finger food: small enough to hold in your hand and eat within a bite or two.

- Cook thoroughly: this generally refers to poultry, beef, and pork. It's essential to cook animal products thoroughly to kill any bacteria in the meat, usually until no pink remains. If you're unsure what this looks like, use a thermometer and follow these approximate guidelines:
  - Poultry cook to 165 degrees
  - Beef cook to 160 degrees
  - Pork cook to 160 degrees

Condiments

- Most store bought condiments contain vegetable/canola oils and a long list of other icky ingredients. To make your own condiments, visit marksdailyapple.com for easy to follow recipes.

- Use avocados in place of creamy condiments like mayo.

- To make Primal whipped cream, add ½ cup (or more) of heavy cream to a blender and whip until it's light and airy.

Proportion Estimates

- 1 cup green salad = baseball
- ½ cup cooked veggies = light bulb
- 1 medium sweet potato = computer mouse
- 1 medium fruit = tennis ball
- 1 oz of cheese = 9-volt battery
- 2 tbsp of nut butter = ping-pong ball
- 3 oz of meat = your palm

Breakfast

You know you've heard the saying, "breakfast is the most important meal of the day," but why? For starters, look at the word itself: break-fast. It's literally the first meal of your day that breaks the overnight fast you've done—so make it count! Breakfast is not the time to load up on sugary cereals or sticky pastries. (Actually there is *never* a time to load up on that junk!) Give your body what it needs to wake up and energize you through the first half of your day.

Perfect Pancakes: Banana or Almond

These are two of my favorite pancake recipes. Not only are they both incredibly easy to make, but they're also delicious and versatile. (You'll see the Banana Pancake recipe pop up again in "Better Than Oatmeal," and the Almond Pancake recipe make an appearance in the "Egg and Cheese McAwesome.")

Makes: 9 pancakes – Time: 15 minutes

Banana Pancake Ingredients
• 1 ripe banana
• 2 eggs
• A pinch of cinnamon
• A splash of vanilla
• Butter (for cooking and topping)
• Optional: fruit, honey, Primal whipped cream (see Condiments on page 193)

Banana Pancake Directions
• Add banana, eggs, cinnamon, and vanilla to a medium bowl and mash together.
• Grease skillet with butter and turn on stove to medium heat.
• Pour batter in skillet to make a three- to four-inch wide pancake.
• Cook until lightly browned on one side, then carefully flip pancake.
• Continue cooking until pancake is cooked throughout.
• Repeat until batter is gone; regreasing skillet between each batch of pancakes.
• Stack pancakes on a plate and top with butter or optional ingredients listed above.

Makes: 3 pancakes – Time: 7 minutes

Almond Pancake Ingredients

- ⅓ cup almond flour
- 1 egg
- A pinch of cinnamon
- A splash of vanilla
- Butter (for cooking and topping)
- Optional: fruit, honey, Primal whipped cream (see Condiments on page 193)

Almond Pancake Directions

- Add almond flour, egg, cinnamon, and vanilla to a medium bowl and mix well.
- Grease skillet with butter and turn on stove to medium heat.
- Pour batter in skillet to make a three- to four-inch wide pancake.
- Cook until lightly browned on one side, then carefully flip pancake.
- Continue cooking until pancake is cooked throughout.
- Repeat until batter is gone; regreasing skillet between each batch of pancakes.
- Stack pancakes on a plate and top with butter or optional ingredients listed above.

Better Than Oatmeal

I stumbled upon this recipe one morning when I was craving Banana Pancakes but didn't feel like standing over the stove pouring and flipping the perfect pancakes over and over—so I just dumped all the batter in the skillet. As I ate my Frankenstein'ed breakfast, I thought it tasted just like oatmeal! The next time I made it, I added nuts and topped it with fruit. From then on, I've been hooked!

Makes: 1 bowl – Time: 5 minutes

Ingredients
- 1 ripe banana
- 2 eggs
- A pinch of cinnamon
- A splash of vanilla
- Butter (for cooking and topping)
- 1-2 tbsp crushed pecans
- Optional: fruit, heavy cream, additional pecans

Directions
- Add banana, eggs, cinnamon, vanilla, and pecans to a medium bowl and mash together; the batter will be a little lumpy.
- Grease skillet with butter and turn on stove to medium heat.
- Add the entire mixture to the skillet.
- As the mixture cooks, continue to stir and mash.
- Once fully cooked, remove from heat and place in a bowl.
- Top with butter or optional ingredients.

Sausage and Sweet Potato Frittata

Frittatas pack a lot of punch! I love making them on a Sunday night, popping them in the fridge, and then heating them up and eating them on the go during the week. They're a perfect finger friendly food for the car or on the bus to school if you're in a time crunch. And if you're anything like me and enjoy eating breakfast any time of day, take them with you for lunch or grab one as an after-school snack.

Makes: 6 slices – Time: 45 minutes

Ingredients
- 1 lb ground pork sausage (or try your favorite meat)
- 6 eggs, scrambled
- 1 medium sweet potato, peeled and diced
- ¼ cup water
- 1 cup spinach, roughly cut
- ⅛ white onion, diced
- 1 tbsp sage
- Seasoning: salt and pepper to taste

Directions
- Preheat the oven to 450 degrees.
- Turn on stove to medium heat, and in an oven-safe skillet, begin cooking sausage, chopping it up as it cooks.
- As the sausage continues cooking, add diced potatos and water.
- Once potatoes are partially cooked, add spinach, onion, sage, salt, and pepper.
- After the spinach is wilted, remove the skillet from heat and add eggs.
- Mix all ingredients in the skillet, then smooth out the mixture so it's distributed evenly. (If your eggs start to cook a bit while you're mixing, that's okay.)
- Bake the frittata in the oven for 15 to 20 minutes or until the eggs are fully cooked and frittata edges are slightly browned.
- Allow frittata to cool for five minutes, then cut into six even slices.
- Refrigerate leftover slices for easy meals on the go.

Egg and Cheese McAwesome

What's better than a plate of fluffy eggs, topped with melted cheese, and a side of warm pancakes? When you stack it together and make a sandwich, of course! This killer sandwich uses the Almond Pancake recipe as the buns and you just fill it with your favorites! This recipe uses egg and cheese, but you could add foods like bacon, sausage, or veggies!

Makes: 1 sandwich – Time: 10 minutes

Ingredients
- ⅓ cup almond flour
- 2 eggs
- 1 slice or 2 oz cheese of your choice
- Butter (for cooking)
- Seasoning: salt and pepper to taste
- Optional: bacon, sausage, sautéed veggies

Directions
- Add almond flour and one egg to a medium bowl and mix well.
- Grease skillet with butter and turn on stove to medium heat.
- Pour batter in skillet making two pancakes of equal size.
- Cook until lightly browned on one side, then carefully flip pancake.
- Continue cooking until pancake is cooked throughout.
- Remove pancakes and regrease skillet.
- Scramble remaining egg, add it to the skillet, and season.
- When the egg is fully cooked, remove the skillet from heat, top with cheese, and cover with lid to allow cheese to melt.
- Place cheesy egg between the two pancakes and add any optional ingredients you'd like.

Paleo Waffles™ and Berries

You'll never believe these giant waffles are 100 percent Primal approved! I discovered these gems from the Julian Bakery and am in love. Not only are they delicious, they're also incredibly filling, and are the perfect meal on mornings when you don't feel like cooking from scratch! Paleo Waffles™ are available online at julianbakery.com or at select stores near you.

Makes: 1 waffle – Time: 20 minutes

Ingredients
- 1 Paleo Waffle™
- ½ cup mixed berries
- Butter
- Optional: honey, Primal whipped cream (see Condiments on page 193)

Directions
- Toast Paleo Waffle™ in toaster. (Or turn oven on to 400 degrees and bake until toasted if it doesn't fit in your toaster...mine doesn't!)
- Cut fruit into bite-sized pieces.
- Top toasted waffle with butter, fruit, or optional ingredients.

Lunch

As a teenager, odds are that five out of seven of your lunches per week are eaten in a cafeteria at school. What does the food look like in your lunch line? Is it full of pizza, french fries, breaded chicken sandwiches, and junk food? Yeah, I figured! Hopefully you pack your lunch and avoid the mystery food being served to you and your classmates. If you haven't made that switch yet, the following recipes should help make the transition a little easier.

Flippin' Chicken Sammie

Who doesn't love a juicy chicken sandwich? It's one of the things I missed the most when I first made the switch to paleo. Instead of letting myself feel deprived, I found a way to fit chicken sandwiches and many other favorites back into my new and healthy lifestyle. All I had to do was *flip* the chicken sandwich inside out!

Makes: 1 sandwich – Time: 20 minutes

Ingredients
- 5 oz chicken breast
- Extra-virgin olive oil (for cooking)
- Seasoning: salt and pepper to taste
- Optional: leafy greens, onion, bacon, avocado, tomato

Directions
- Oil the skillet with extra-virgin olive oil and turn on stove to medium heat.
- Season chicken breast and add to skillet.
- Cook chicken thoroughly, until there isn't any pink left inside.
- Allow chicken to cool enough to handle.
- Cut chicken breast in half making two "chicken buns."
- Add optional toppings between the two pieces of chicken.
- For on-the-go sammies, wrap in foil and eat "burrito-style" to minimize mess.

Once again, the culinary geniuses from Julian Bakery knew the way to my heart: Paleo Wraps™. These wraps are so versatile! I've used them for everything from breakfast quesadillas, to almond butter and jam rollups, to the tacos I'm sharing with you here. This is probably one of my favorite recipes to make, so beware their deliciousness! Paleo Wraps™ are available online at julianbakery.com or at select stores near you.

Makes: 2 tacos – Time: 5 minutes

Ingredients
- ¼ lb ground beef (or one frozen hamburger patty)
- 2 Paleo Wraps™
- 1 oz cheese of your choice
- Seasoning: salt, garlic powder, and chili powder to taste
- Optional: leafy greens, salsa, onions, tomato, sour cream, guacamole, fresh squeezed lime juice

Directions
- Turn on stove to medium-high heat and add beef and seasoning to your skillet.
- Cook beef until fully browned, chopping it up as it cooks.
- Split beef in half and add portions to each wrap.
- Top with cheese and optional toppings.

Leftover Makeover Salad

It's 8:00 pm on a Wednesday night. You and your parents just spent the past two hours cooking (and more importantly, eating) the biggest and most amazing Primal dinner you've had in weeks. Now that you're coming down from your foodie-high, all you can think about is the giant mess you have to clean up, the homework you still need to finish, and the fact that you still have to pack your lunch for tomorrow! But have no fear; this super simple salad using leftovers from dinner will make cleanup a breeze and your lunch a piece of cake. Well, not literally.

Makes: 1 salad – Time: 10 minutes

Ingredients
- 5 oz leftover meat, chopped
- 1 ½ cups leafy greens
- ½ cup fresh veggies of your choice (or grilled leftovers)
- Optional: cheese or nuts
- Dressing: olive oil and vinegar, ranch from page 227, or half an avocado (in place of dressing)

Directions
- In a reusable container, add leafy greens, veggies, and leftover meat.
- If using cheese or nuts, you may want to store them in a separate container to keep them from getting soggy.
- Keep olive oil and vinegar in a separate container until you're ready to eat.
- Keep avocado wrapped in plastic wrap to prevent browning.
- When it's time to eat, toss all of your ingredients together.

Roasted Tomato Soup

Sometimes the perfect cup of soup not only hits the spot in your belly, but also in your heart. It's like a warm hug in a bowl. It's like a snuggly blanket fresh out of the dryer. It's like cuddling with your adorable puppy. Ok, that's plenty of soup analogies…you get the picture. This is by far my favorite soup to make on days when it's a little chilly, or if I just want some serious comfort food.

Makes: 6 servings – Time: 1 hour 30 minutes

Ingredients
- 6 large tomatoes
- 3 garlic cloves
- A handful of basil
- 4 tbsp extra-virgin olive oil
- Seasoning: salt and pepper to taste
- Optional: for a little kick, add a couple jalapeños or serrano chilies

Directions
- Preheat oven to 375 degrees.
- Chop tomatoes, garlic, and basil, and place in an oven safe baking dish.
- Drizzle the chopped veggies with extra-virgin olive oil and salt and pepper
- Cover baking dish with foil and bake for one hour.
- Remove the tomatoes from the oven very carefully; the dish will be full of boiling liquid that you can't see beneath the foil.
- Allow tomatoes to cool for 15 or 20 minutes to make them easier to handle.
- Pour tomatoes and all contents of the dish into a blender and blend until liquid is smooth.
- Eat immediately and refrigerate/freeze remaining soup in single-serving, reusable containers for easily reheatable meals.

Dinner

Breakfast, check. Lunch, check. Now it's time for dinner. This is your last chance to get all your veggies, protein, and healthy fats in for the day before you begin to wind down and start your overnight fast—so make it count! Depending on how late it is (and how early you plan on catching some zzzs) you might not need a giant portion for dinner. Sometimes eating a smaller serving for your last meal, and adding a salad for some bonus veggies, is all you need to round out your day. Just listen to your body.

Cave Crave Pizza

Okay, let's be real. Most teenagers would gladly live off pizza exclusively. Heck, some probably do. And since you've made the Primal leap, you've probably caught yourself daydreaming of a hot slice every once in a while, right? Well, today is your lucky day, my friend! Primal pizza is a real thing. Sometimes I even whip up a couple of these crusts, cut them down to size, and freeze them for later use. Prepping in bulk seriously makes life so much easier!

Makes: 8 servings – Time: 40 minutes

Ingredients for Crust
- 2 cups almond flour
- 1 cup arrowroot flour
- 1 tsp baking powder
- Seasoning: 1 tsp salt, 1 tsp oregano
- 3 eggs
- ½ cup almond milk

Ingredients for toppings
- Whatever you like: sauce, cheese, veggies, and meat

Directions
- Preheat oven to 425 degrees.
- Combine dry ingredients in a large bowl.
- Add eggs and almond milk to dry mixture.
- On a greased baking sheet, spread batter with spatula (batter will be runny and not the consistancy of typical pizza dough).
- Bake for 10 minutes or until lightly browned.
- Remove crust from oven and top with your favorite toppings.
- Bake for an additional 10 minutes or until cheese is melted.

Inside-Out-Burger and Sweetie Fries

Happiness is a cheeseburger and fries. And just like you don't want to feel deprived from pizza, odds are you don't want to feel deprived from this all-American favorite either. With this recipe we're tossing the bun, turning this sucker inside out, and giving those pale, boring fries a tan.

Makes: 1 burger and 1 serving of fries – Time: 30 minutes

Ingredients for fries
- 1 small sweet potato
- 1-2 tbsp coconut oil (for cooking)
- Seasoning: salt and pepper, and chili powder to taste

Directions for fries
- Slice potato into long, ¼ inch thick pieces. (You can do this with skin on or off.)
- Turn stove on to medium-high heat and melt coconut oil in medium skillet.
- Add potatoes to skillet and sprinkle with seasoning.
- If the potatoes soak up all the coconut oil, add more to the skillet so they don't burn.
- Cook for about 15 to 17 minutes or until the fries are tender and slightly browned.

Ingredients for burger
- 5 oz ground beef
- 1 oz cheese of your choice
- 2 leaves of lettuce
- Optional: tomato, onion, pickle, avocado, bacon
- Seasoning: salt and pepper

Directions for burger
- While the fries are cooking, split the meat in half and make two thin patties.
- Ball cheese up, place it between the two burger patties. Pinch the edges shut, sealing the cheese inside, then season the burger.
- In a small skillet, turn on stove to medium heat and cook the burger covered for about five to seven minutes on each side or until cooked thoroughly.
- If the cheese oozes out while you're cooking the burger, just top it with more cheese and allow it to melt for a few minutes after the beef is fully cooked.
- Top burger with your favorite extras and use lettuce leaves as buns.

Comfy Crockpot Stew

Crockpots, or slow cookers, aren't just for Grandma. You'll flip when you see how easy it is to make a legit dinner in one of these bad boys! Not to mention, you'll earn mega bonus points from your parents when they realize you have dinner ready when they get home from work.

Makes: 6 servings – Time: 5 hours 15 minutes (or up to 8 hours)

Ingredients
- 2 lbs chuck roast
- 1 cup water or stock (any kind)
- 1 cup carrots
- 2 cups celery
- ½ onion
- 1 medium sweet potato (peeled or unpeeled)
- 3 garlic cloves, minced
- 1 tbsp sage
- Seasoning: salt and pepper to taste
- Optional: your favorite veggies, if they weren't already listed

Directions
- Place meat in crockpot and top with sage, salt, and pepper.
- Add water or stock.
- Dice all veggies to bite-sized pieces and add to crockpot.
- Top with additional salt and pepper and cover.
- Cook for about five hours on high (or eight hours on low if you'll be gone all day) or until meat is cooked through and veggies are tender.
- Store leftovers in single-serving, reusable containers for on-the-go meals.

Easy Wings with Veggies and Ranch

You don't need to be at a party to have wings and chow down on a veggie tray! You can turn any regular weekday into a celebration and whip this meal up in no time. Besides, nothing beats the crispy skin and juicy meat of a well-cooked chicken wing. My mouth is watering just thinking about wings!

Makes: 2 servings – Time: 1 hour 10 minutes

Wings Ingredients
- 1 lb trimmed chicken wings
- 1 tbsp each: chili powder, sage
- Seasoning: salt and pepper to taste

Wings Directions
- Preheat oven to 375 degrees.
- Season chicken wings with chili powder, sage, salt, and pepper.
- Place on foil-lined baking sheet or glass baking dish and bake for one hour or until cooked thoroughly and skin is crispy, flipping wings once at 30 minutes.

Veggies and Ranch Ingredients
- Optional veggies: baby carrots, broccoli, cauliflower, bell peppers, cherry tomatoes
- 8 oz sour cream
- 1 tsp each: parsley, onion (minced), dill
- Garlic powder and salt to taste

Veggies and Ranch Directions
- Begin preparing the veggies and ranch while the wings are in the oven.
- Slice all veggies into "finger food" sized portions.
- Combine sour cream and seasoning in a bowl.
- Refrigerate the veggies and ranch until the wings are done.

Snacks

One of the coolest things you'll notice once you fully adapt to Primal eating habits is the transition from being a sugar burner to a fat burner. That's when your body stops using the glucose/sugar in your bloodstream for energy and starts metabolizing your stored fat for energy instead. When you're a fat burner, you feel fuller for longer and don't feel like you need to snack every couple of hours. Of course there will be days that for some reason your body just needs more fuel; maybe you had to walk to your friend's house a few miles away to study for a final, or your coach made you swim extra laps at practice, or you could be going through a growth spurt. Regardless of the reason, your body is demanding more energy, so listen to it! With these quick and easy snacks, you and your tummy will be happy in no time.

Deli Rollups

Get the protein punch of a deli sandwich without all the bread. You can knock these rollups out in seconds and they really hit the spot. Primal tip: when hunting for deli meats at the grocery, look for nitrate-free, minimally processed meats, or make your own deli meat at home and slice it super thin!

Makes: 3 roll-ups – Time: 10 minutes

Ingredients
- 3-6 slices of your favorite deli meats (depending on the size of the slices, or around 3 oz total): ham, turkey, salami, chicken, roast beef, etc.
- 1 slice or 3 oz cheese of your choice, cut into thirds
- Optional: avocado, tomato, leaf lettuce, onion, salt, pepper, and any of your favorite veggies, herbs, or seasonings

Directions
- Lay meat slices out side by side, or use leaf lettuce as a "wrap."
- Place a piece of cheese in the center of each meat.
- Add any optional ingredients.
- Roll up into finger friendly snacks.

Banana Bites

In the mood for something that's sweet and savory? These addictive little snacks will satisfy your sweet tooth with natural sweetness.

Makes: 1 serving – Time: 3 minutes

Ingredients
- 1 banana (the riper it is, the sweeter it will be)
- 3 tbsp almond butter
- Seasoning: salt and cinnamon to taste

Directions
- Peel banana and cut into ½ inch slices.
- Arrange banana slices on a plate and lightly salt.
- Top each banana with a small dollop of almond butter.
- Sprinkle with cinnamon.

Primal Fuel

For instances when you don't have time to cook (or even eat for that matter), or maybe you're just in the mood for something that's a little more dessert-like, drink a protein shake! When you're on the go, protein shakes can be as convenient as just adding a scoop or two of protein powder and some water to your blender bottle, or you can go super gourmet and make a fancy smoothie. While there are a lot of protein shakes on the market, beware of those made with health-compromising substances like: GMO's, growth hormone rBGH, soy, artificial sweeteners, heavy metals, antibiotics, or anything whose name you can't pronounce. My favorite Primal-approved go-to is Primal Fuel. You can get this tasty beverage in flavors like Chocolate Coconut or Vanilla Coconut Crème in 15 or 30 serving sizes at primalblueprint.com.

Makes: 1 shake – Time: 3 minutes

Simple Vanilla Shake Ingredients
- 2 scoops of Vanilla Coconut Crème Primal Fuel
- 8-10 oz cold water
- Optional: ice

Simple Vanilla Shake Directions
- Add items to a blender bottle and shake well.

Banana Bread Smoothie* Ingredients
- 2 scoops of Chocolate Coconut Primal Fuel
- 4 oz cold water, 1/2 cup of ice
- ½ frozen banana
- ½ tsp cinnamon

Banana Bread Smoothie Directions
- Add items to a blender and process until smooth.

* Many more Primal Fuel recipes available at primalblueprint.com

Grab-N-Go's

When in doubt, keep snacks simple. Some of the easiest and healthiest meals are single ingredient foods. If the simplicity of this has you stumped, here are some Primal-approved foods you can literally throw into a plastic baggy or reusable container and be on your way:

- Hard boiled egg
- Baby carrots
- Raw almonds
- String cheese
- Strawberries
- Broccoli
- Cottage cheese
- Raw macadamia nuts
- Raspberries
- Apple
- Beef jerky
- Full-fat Greek yogurt
- Orange
- Scoop of almond butter
- Banana
- Cold chicken leg
- Avocado
- Cucumber slices
- Cherries
- Dark chocolate (70 percent or higher)

What other single ingredient snack items can you come up with?

Beauty Products

Since you don't want to put junk in your body, you shouldn't put junk *on* your body either. After all, your skin is your largest organ and anything you slather onto it absorbs right into your body. If you wouldn't eat it, don't use it! Finding the perfect product that meets your paleo needs and doesn't break the bank can be tough. That's why I've developed some killer homemade products that won't cost you a million bucks, but will certainly make you look like a million bucks.

Coconut Milk All-Over Wash

This versatile wash can be used from head to toe. Add some to a bath sponge and cover yourself in its milky bubbles, massage it onto your face for a moisturizing face wash, or use 1 to 2 tablespoons of it in your hair (depending how long your hair is) for an all-natural shampoo. For an added kick, mix in 5 drops of peppermint oil and experience a tingly fresh feeling that's super cool.

Ingredients
- ½ cup coconut milk
- ⅔ cup castile soap
- 1 tsp preferred oil (vitamin E, olive, almond, coconut)
- Optional: 5 drops preferred essential oil for fragrance (eucalyptus, rose, lavender)

Directions
- Mix all ingredients and store in a resealable bottle, labeled with the date.
- Shake the container well before each use to combine ingredients that separate.
- Store in your shower for up to one month.

Dry Shampoos

Whether you're trying to shampoo less, don't want your color to fade, or occasionally don't have time to wash and dry your hair, dry shampoo can be a blessing in a bottle. There are plenty of products on the market that take the oil out of your hair, but most of them also dry out your hair in the process, are full of chemicals, and can be expensive. The following are some simple, one- or two-ingredient dry shampoo replacements with items you probably already have in your kitchen!

Dry Shampoo Replacements
- Baby powder
- Cornstarch
- 1 tbsp salt, ½ cup cornmeal
- ½ cup ground oatmeal, ½ cup baking soda
- ½ cup baking soda, ½ cup baby powder

Dry Shampoo Directions (same for all)
- For single ingredient replacements, use as is. For two-ingredient replacements, mix thoroughly.
- Begin with clean hands because oils from your hands will transfer to your hair.
- Use a small shaker, clean makeup brush, or your fingertips to apply powder to oily areas (mostly close to the scalp and roots).
- Use fingertips or makeup brush to rub powder into hair and scalp.
- Brush hair to remove any powder that didn't get absorbed.
- Clean hair brush and/or makeup brush after use to prevent powder buildup.

Facial Cleansers

Odds are that your paleo lifestyle is already helping the condition of your skin. When you eat right, your skin is at its healthiest. Breakouts diminish, splotchy patches fade, and you look radiant. That doesn't mean your face doesn't need to be washed anymore! Check out these all-natural facial cleansers that are, you guessed it, probably in your kitchen already!

Honey Facial Cleanser Directions – best for normal skin
- Rub 1 tsp honey in the palm of your hands, or if wearing makeup, squeeze honey onto washcloth and mix with a little baking soda.
- Massage honey into face for a minute or two.
- Rinse with warm water.
- Tip: add 1 tsp cream for dry skin or 1 tsp lemon juice for oily skin.

Oil Facial Cleanser – best for combination skin
- Rub 1 tbsp of oil (castor, olive, coconut, jojoba, or combination) in the palm of your hand.
- Massage oil into your skin for a minute or two.
- Hold a hot washcloth on your face for 20 seconds, then wipe off remaining oil.
- If your face feels dry, just rub a drop of the same oil across the tight area.
- Tip: remember from chemistry class, "like dissolves like," meaning that oil dissolves oil—so don't be intimidated by oil cleansing.

Yogurt Facial Cleanser – best for dry skin
- Apply 1 tbsp of plain yogurt across your face.
- Massage yogurt into your skin for a minute or two.
- Rinse with warm water.
- Tip: add 1 tsp lemon juice or a drop or two of essential oil for a sweet smelling cleanser.

Primal tip: If you want a tougher scrub, add a pinch of cornmeal to any of the facial cleansers above for a little extra grit.

Moisturizer

If you're anything like me and moisturize daily, you'd better be sure you're rubbing something of quality into your skin. Like all other beauty products, there are enough lotions on the market to make your head spin. There are also a ton of DIY recipes online to make your own lotions using a bunch of different ingredients, but by now I bet you've caught on to the fact that minimal ingredients (for food and beauty products) are the way to go. So I'm going to make this really simple for you. Are you ready for this? The number one, all-natural, single item you should use as a moisturizer is: *coconut oil.* Surprised? Yeah, probably not at this point!

Coconut Oil Moisturizer tips and directions

- For sanitary purposes, keep two jars of coconut oil in your home at all times: one in the kitchen, and one in the bathroom.
- Coconut oil is solid at below 78 degrees, and liquid above that temperature.
- Keeping coconut oil in the shower can help it attain its liquid state and make for easy application as a moisturizer after bathing. (Be sure to clean your shower floor regularly so it doesn't get slippery and don't let a bunch go down the drain since it could clog it!)
- Coconut oil can also be used as a hair moisturizer by applying it in a liquid form to hair tips, then shampooing it out after an hour.
- Use as an "Oil Facial Cleanser" (see page 245) and a facial moisturizer for its natural antibacterial, antifungal, and antiviral properties against acne and eczema.
- Apply it to dry or chapped lips to nourish and heal.
- Hydrate your cuticles by using coconut oil as a cuticle treatment.
- Keep legs smooth and conditioned by using coconut oil as a shaving cream.
- Use a drop or two of coconut oil in your hair to smooth flyaways and dry frizz.

Glossary

Anorexia is a type of eating disorder that occurs when individuals severely restrict their food intake, often to the point of starvation. More symptoms of anorexia are distorted body image, irrational fear of weight gain, and an obsession with being thin.

Antioxidants can be found in certain fruits and vegetables, and play their part by helping the cells in your body fight disease and infection.

Breathing isn't just an involuntary action. During exercise it's crucial to perform proper breathing technique—never hold your breath! Holding your breath cuts oxygen off from your muscles and brain, and could cause you to become dizzy or faint. If you're doing cardio, practice deep "belly" breathing into your diaphragm. If you're lifting heavy weight (or your own body weight), always exhale on the effort and inhale when you're returning to your starting position. If you're stretching or doing yoga, practice deep breathing like you would with cardio, but to an even slower degree.

Bulimia is a type of eating disorder characterized by the pattern of binge eating and then purging. Binge eating is ingesting a large amount of food in a short period of time and then forcing regurgitation of that food by intentional vomiting or through the use of a laxative or diuretic.

Burnout occurs when you physically or mentally collapse because you're overstressed or overworked (over-exercising).

Cage-free/free-range is a label that refers to poultry products produced by chickens that were not confined to cases and were given access to the outside. This designation, however, doesn't specify how long each day the chickens had access to the outdoors, or that they were even aware they could roam. They could still be kept in cramped, confined, unclean living quarters without ever seeing the outdoors their entire lives.

Chronic cardio describes a workout conducted at medium-high intensity for too long and too frequently. Because chronic cardio is a form of over-exercising, it does more harm than good.

Circadian rhythm is the internal 24-hour cycle that regulates eating and sleeping patterns, hormone releases, brain wave patterns, and cellular repair and regeneration.

Commercial/conventional food consisting of vegetables, fruit, meat, and fowl, is produced by "commercial/conventional" farms across the world. However, these farms usually don't adhere to organic and grass-fed standards, so tons of chemicals like pesticides are used on the fruits and vegetables, and the animals are forced to live in unnatural ways (e.g., forcing animals to eat double the quantity of food they would eat in their natural habitat—like corn—and not allowing the animals to go outside/leave their cages).

Conventional wisdom refers to ideas or explanations that are typically accepted as truth by the public, regardless of their actual validity.

Cortisol is the stress hormone that makes you crave sugar and store fat.

Crossfit is a fitness program that revolves around a specific exercise philosophy. At Crossfit, people do Olympic weightlifting, high-intensity interval training, powerlifting, gymnastics, calisthenics, and strongman exercises.

Dynamic stretching is stretching while you're moving. Because active movement is required for dynamic stretching, it is particularly beneficial when performed before lifting weights, playing sports, or as a pre-workout in general.

Estrogen is a hormone that is responsible for developing and maintaining the female characteristics that happen in (and to) your body, such as menstruation and pregnancy.

Farmers markets are open-air markets where you can buy organic food from local farms. The prices are usually the same as grocery store prices, and the quality is usually superior!

Flexibility is the range in which your muscles can stretch without strain. Flexibility can be improved through exercise and stretching.

Freshman 15 refers to the fact that many freshmen in college tend to gain weight—usually around an extra 15 pounds. Those extra 15 pounds typically result from excess carbohydrate, processed food, and alcohol consumption, as well as lack of exercise.

Glycemic value/level refers to the sugar content of food. A food with a high glycemic value causes your blood sugar to spike, giving your body an unstable source of energy, aka a "sugar high."

Genetically modified organisms (GMOS) can be found in the majority of processed and packaged food, but are also put in tampons and pads.

Grains and starches are found in barley, corn, oats, rice, rye, and wheat.

Grass-fed animals are raised on a foraged diet, instead of being fed grains and other "food" that is unnatural to them and difficult for their bodies to digest.

Grokette is our model of the average girl living 10,000 years ago. She didn't have an iPhone or a Facebook, but she was healthy and very active!

Healthy "good" fats come from food sources like avocados, egg yolks, coconut oil, and olive oil. They are a critical part of keeping your body healthy, and help you absorb crucial vitamins like A, D, E, and K.

High-intensity interval training (HIIT) consists of brief but intense workouts that last anywhere from 4-30 minutes. They increase your athletic aptitude, improve your glucose metabolism, and boost your ability to burn fat.

Insulin is a hormone produced in the pancreas that regulates the amount of glucose in your blood. It plays a crucial role in regulating carbohydrate and fat metabolism in your body.

Ketones are compounds produced by your body when it burns fat stores for energy instead of carbs. This is referred to as being in a state of ketosis or keto. When your diet is very low in carbs, your body produces ketones out of fatty acids in your liver, and uses ketones as your body's principal source of energy.

Legumes are beans, lentils, chickpeas, split peas, and soybeans.

Melatonin is a hormone that regulates your sleep cycles.

Mobility is the degree to which your joints can move without strain. Doing mobility work daily is important because if you don't, you can develop connective tissue and calcium deposits in the wrong places, a condition that is permanent. You're also more prone to injuries if you lose mobility in your joints, so it's essential to maintain your mobility by moving your joints every day.

Omega-3s are polyunsaturated fatty acids that can be found in fish, flax, algae, and nuts. They are anti-inflammatory, support healthy brain function, and aid in decreasing symptoms of depression and anxiety.

Omega-6s are unsaturated fatty acids that can be found in corn and various grains. In moderation they are essential for renal function and dermal integrity. However, watch the ratio between your omega-6 and omega-3 intake, as an abundance of omega-6s promotes inflammation. A 1:1 ratio of omega-6 to omega-3 fatty acids is highly recommended.

Organic foods and products are not exposed to chemicals like pesticides and are therefore treated as naturally as possible.

Organically raised animals eat organic food and are not given drugs, antibiotics, or growth hormones.

Oxybenzone is a chemical that provides protection from the sun. Its safety level is questionable, so try to stay away from this ingredient when choosing a SPF.

Paleo/Primal refers to a lifestyle that seeks to mimic the lives of our ancestors by consuming healthy fats, avoiding processed food, and being active, among many other key concepts.

Pasture-raised animals roam freely in their natural environment and consume a natural diet. Pasturing improves the welfare of the animal, helps reduce environmental damage, and yields higher quality products that taste better and are more nutritious than conventional products. This is the label you should be looking for!

Pesticides/herbicides are chemicals that are sprayed on plants to kill bugs and weeds but end up soaking into and contaminating the produce.

Processed food is created from unnatural processes, and therefore is horrible for your body and your metabolism. Bread, cake, cereal, cookies, crackers, pasta, and soda are just a few examples of processed food.

Proprioception is crucial to exercising well because it is responsible for your awareness of your body in space and time. When you're doing a flip or a cartwheel, proprioception tells your hands, feet, arms, etc. where to be so you can complete the move successfully and safely.

Saturated fats are healthy (despite conventional wisdom declaring otherwise) and are found in animal protein and dairy, as well as fruits like avocados and coconuts. They aid in calcium absorption and support immune function, and are an impressive source of fat-soluble vitamins. However, they can cause damage when paired with processed carbs.

Sedentary lifestyle describes a lifestyle marked by physical inactivity. Someone who is not physically active, or is only infrequently physically active, lives a sedentary lifestyle.

Standard American Diet (SAD) refers to the typical diet of the average American. This diet is comprised of 15 percent protein, 50 percent carbohydrate, and 35 percent fat. The SAD is strongly linked to high obesity levels, as well as death from heart disease, cancer, and other illnesses.

Static stretching is stretching while your body is resting. It requires less active movement than dynamic stretching does, increases flexibility, and is very helpful when performed post-workout.

Unhealthy "bad" fats come from processed, synthetic, and manufactured foods, like cake, cookies, crackers, etc. They mess with your metabolism, increase inflammation, promote weight gain, speed up the aging process, and cause cancer.

Unhealthy "bad" carbs spike your insulin, increase inflammation, make you a couch potato, can trigger depression, and directly cause weight gain.

UV (UVB) radiation causes more superficial damage to your skin, like sunburn and skin reddening, but also plays a large role in cancer development. Safe exposure to UVB rays is crucial to maintaining healthy vitamin D levels.

UVA rays are ultraviolet rays from the sun that cause damage to the skin. They penetrate into your skin more powerfully than UVB light, so they cause long-term damage to your skin—like wrinkles and sunspots (brown spots), and more seriously, cancer.

Vitamin D is a hormone that is important for healthy bones, teeth, and nails, good eyesight, absorption of vitamins, and a healthy immune system. Vitamin D lowers your chances of developing certain diseases and inflammatory conditions. You can get your required dosage of vitamin D from sun exposure and from food like eggs, salmon, and cod liver oil.

Wild-caught refers to fish that isn't cultivated in farms/compact tanks. Wild-caught fish are raised and caught in their natural habitat.

Yo-yo dieting is when people switch from diet to diet in the hopes of finding the perfect one that will help them lose weight and improve their health. What most people don't realize is that they don't need a diet—they need a lifestyle change, like going Primal/Paleo, in order to truly transform their health and their body for the better.

Zinc oxide is an ingredient that you should look for when choosing a sunscreen because it's a natural, safe, and efficient form of physical protection from the sun. It is also safe for sensitive skin.

For a complete list of references used for the writing of *Paleo Girl,* please visit: primalblueprintpublishing.com/paleo-girl-references/